# LIVING WITH THE
# 1911

*If you wish to become a really good shot you will learn to live with your gun.*

—Col. Jeff Cooper

*Every 10 years the .45 becomes fashionable again.*

—Louis Awerbuck

*Your heart is where the warrior resides.*

—Morgan W. Boatman

# LIVING WITH THE
# 1911

## A Fresh Look at the Fighting Gun

### ROBERT H. BOATMAN

PALADIN PRESS • BOULDER, COLORADO

**Also by Robert Boatman:**

Living with Glocks:
    The Complete Guide to the New Standard in Combat Handguns
Living with the Big .50:
    The Shooter's Guide to the World's Most Powerful Rifle

*Living with the 1911: A Fresh Look at the Fighting Gun*
by Robert H. Boatman

Copyright © 2005 by Robert H. Boatman

ISBN 10:  1-58160-467-X
ISBN 13:  978-1-58160-467-2
Printed in the United States of America

Published by Paladin Press, a division of
Paladin Enterprises, Inc.
Gunbarrel Tech Center
7077 Winchester Circle
Boulder, Colorado 80301 USA
+1.303.443.7250

Direct inquiries and/or orders to the above address.

PALADIN, PALADIN PRESS, and the "horse head" design
are trademarks belonging to Paladin Enterprises and
registered in United States Patent and Trademark Office.

Visit our Web site at www.paladin-press.com

Cover photo: Morgan W. Boatman

# Contents

For my grandfather and his well-used Colts.

# Special Thanks

Morgan W. Boatman

Dave Brennan
Editor-in-Chief, *The Accurate Rifle*

The National Rifle Association
The nation's oldest and largest civil rights organization

Tactical Firearms Training Team

Yavapai Firearms Academy

Gunsite Academy

Sconce

Interview Subjects, 1911 People, and Friends:
Louis Awerbuck
Robbie Barrkman
Jeff Cooper
Max Joseph
Wayne Novak
Gary Reeder
Kase Reeder
Terry Tussey

# Preface
## Thanks, Dick

I got my first .45 automatic when I was 6 years old. It was a birthday present and came in a blue cardboard box wrapped in shiny red paper with a fancy white bow on it. There were other things in that package, but their appeal was limited. The wristwatch radio and silver Dick Tracy shield soon went the way of all dull playthings, but the big, black, slab-sided pistol remained a trusty companion for years. I didn't know it was supposed to be John Browning's Model of 1911; I knew it as a .45 automatic. That's what we called them then, at least in Texas. That was the magic phrase. And I knew it went BOOM, or sometimes BLAM, occasionally CRACK, but never just BANG, as that was the sound little .38 revolvers made. I carried that .45 automatic until I was too old to play with toy guns. And then I replaced it with a real one.

There was a guy named Eric in high school who always carried a .45 automatic, carried it stuck in his belt under his shirt, hammer down on a live round. He liked to cock the hammer back slowly right next to his ear so he could hear all the musical clicks his sear spring made. Eric was two years older than I was, but we were in the same class. He was the leader of a local gang, and after we'd pounded each other to a bloody standstill in a marathon fistfight one day, we became friends. We would cut classes all the time and go out in his lowered black Mercury coupe and shoot his .45. Eric shot a whitetail doe with it once and she dropped like a feed sack.

In college, I pawned my Selmer tenor saxophone to buy an Argentine Ballester-Molina. I carried it in the waistband of my pants under my shirt, cocked and locked. I didn't know that was the way you were supposed to carry a 1911; I just enjoyed the effect the cocked hammer had on my gun-ignorant East Coast Yankee classmates. Their eyes couldn't have opened wider and their conversations wouldn't have stopped more abruptly if they had suddenly noticed that I wasn't wearing any pants at all. When the dean gave me the choice of getting rid of my .45 or clearing out of school, I naturally shoved a spare magazine in my pocket and headed west.

A childhood friend wanted me to team up with him and join the police force. I thought I might, until I learned that cops had to carry .38 Specials. Later on, out in Los Angeles, when I was in a position to write my own ticket, I agreed to do some undercover work as a reserve officer on the condition that I could carry whatever I wanted. When I became a plainclothes sergeant and was responsible for conducting oral exams with officer candidates, I developed the habit of removing my jacket in the midst of the interview to reveal a chrome-plated, ivory-handled 1911 hanging heavily under my arm in a shoulder rig. I would ask the recruit what he thought he might do if I suddenly drew that .45 and blew his partner's head off. It was a question to which there was no correct answer, but there were plenty of character-revealing stabs at it.

Along the way, I studied and practiced Col. Jeff Cooper's Modern Technique of the Pistol under Max Joseph at TFTT (Tactical Firearms Training Team) in California and have since had enlightening conversations with the colonel himself about the philosophical foundation of his revolutionary doctrine. Cooper is more closely

associated with the 1911 than anyone except Browning. Indeed, in the context of this book, it is Cooper rather than Browning who is a constant presence and guiding spirit. It was Cooper who recognized why Browning designed the 1911 the way he did, who saw and understood the depths of the gun, who guided the development of the most effective techniques to take advantage of Browning's invention. Colonel Cooper made it his life's work to teach professionals and amateurs alike how best to deploy the 1911—strategically, tactically, and mechanically. In the process, he redefined and advanced combat and defensive marksmanship for all time. He crystallized important concepts and principles according to which the lives of modern warriors could properly be lived. Colonel Cooper, far more than any other player in the great 1911 drama, assured the future of the 1911 as the pistol that will live forever. Thanks, Jeff.

In my own decades of living with the 1911, I've used the pistol for just about everything a pistol can be used for. I have always and will continue to carry a .45 for personal protection and for the protection of those around me. Even if I had not made a lot of treacherous enemies in my life, which I have, I would carry a pistol because I recognize that it is my social obligation to do so. It is perhaps my only social obligation. Like most gun people, a highly independent and liberty-loving lot, I expect society in general to get along all right without much help from me, and me without much help from it.

# Introduction
## Once Upon a Time in the West

John Browning of Utah might as well have invented the plow. In its own way, his big-bore semiautomatic pistol has been responsible for feeding and otherwise sustaining almost as many people. We call Browning's .45 automatic the 1911 because that's the year it was first adopted by the U.S. Army, but that was only the beginning of a very long story.

The first 1911 came out of the Colt factory when my long-lived and long-dead grandfather was a very young man. The year Roy Rogers was born. And Jean Harlow. And Ronald Reagan. When England had a king and Irishman John Rigby devised his 416-caliber Mauser-action rifle and first class U.S. postage was 2 cents. Most cars—the few there were—had to be hand-cranked to start and ran only a short time before breaking down, which didn't much matter because rush-hour horse traffic was intolerable, and there were few roads outside the city limits anyway. The Belfast-built hull of the *Titanic* was launched and the 10-month fitting-out process begun, but they hadn't hired a dance band yet. There was no television. Think of that, no television. The entire left-wing media machine was just an evil sparkle in some subversive academic's eyes. It was the year they first danced the Charleston in Charleston.

Undoubtedly, this was all way before your time. Ancient history. But, as every person who's lived about a third of a century knows, history has a way of repeating itself.

Today, resting on the desk beside my computer in its definitive cocked-and-locked, ready-for-anything condition is a brand new 1911 that was proudly turned out by a promising young gunsmith just last week.

The computer, which didn't even exist in anybody's imagination that many years ago, provides instantaneous communication between just about every gun designer in the world. Everyone has immediate access to virtually all the information amassed since the beginning of recorded history. You can draw a three-dimensional gun on your computer screen, plug it into a powerful CNC machine, and watch all that computer-driven machinery carve the gun of your dreams out of solid steel. In this day and age, if there were any improvements to be made in the basic design of the 1911, the guy next door could do it in his garage. There are plenty of those guys turning out new 1911s just the way Browning designed the original, because none of them has managed to improve it.

This new 1911 sitting here, other than surface cosmetics, minor variations in the shape of a few external parts, and perhaps stronger steel, is the same gun John Browning designed and Colt produced nearly a hundred years ago. The gun was modular before the term modular was ever used, so anybody can replace any given part with another of a somewhat different shape, finish, look, or feel, but always the same function. The design has not changed in any material way whatsoever in almost a century. There are not many products about which anything like that can be said.

It's extremely difficult, if not patently impossible, to improve on the few timeless tools that were designed to perform an essential and fundamental job in the most simple and straightforward manner—the ax, the claw hammer, the plow, the .45 automatic. The march of the 1911 pistol through history is marked not by major design changes but by momentous events.

### 1902

Perhaps you doubt that history repeats itself.
On July 4, 1902, President Theodore Roosevelt declared the Philippines War officially over. Except, of course, "in the country inhabited by the Moro tribes." The Moros, so called by the Spanish, were 35,000 fanatical Islamic warriors, Muslim terrorists if you will, who "fought in the way of Allah" and declared a jihad, or holy war, against American infidels. The Moros were a small, fierce people with no fear of dying. One of the few things they feared was that their families

would survive them, so they often charged into certain death holding their children in front of them as shields. With almost unstoppable bullet-eating assaults, booby trap warfare as sophisticated and deadly as in Vietnam, and suicidal attacks reminiscent of the Middle East today, the Moros kept more than one-fifth of the U.S. Army fully occupied for a decade.

With hair and eyebrows shaved; arteries and genitals bound in leather to slow the flow of blood and deaden the sensation of pain; drugged out of their minds on who-knows-what; and armed mostly with spears, hatchets, daggers, and swords, plus a few old Arab matchlocks and ancient flintlocks dating to the American Revolution and the Southern War for Independence, the Moros made superhuman efforts to fulfill their oaths to kill (and eat) Christians in order to assure their places in paradise.

Moro invincibility was legendary. In one instance, a Moro warrior received 14 bullet wounds in five minutes, three of which penetrated his brain, and yet he fought on. As one seasoned army officer told a reporter, "Even the veteran Indian fighters among [the army regulars] had to learn that a Moro was more dangerous than a renegade Apache and twice as hard to kill." Newspaper accounts of the time were filled with such reports. Col. Louis LaGarde writes in *Gunshot Injuries*, published in 1916, that he received countless letters from the battlefield attesting to the Moros' virtual invincibility. The arrival of the new Colt semiautomatic pistols in 1911 was welcome, as this account of the death of a Moro warrior by an American soldier attests: "He had 32 Krag balls through him and was only stopped by the 33rd bullet—a Colt .45 slug through both ears."

In 1913 some semblance of peace prevailed, but the Moros were never permanently subdued. In fact, in 1972, they rebelled again when martial law was declared in the Philippines and the government ordered civilians to surrender their guns. The right to keep and bear arms is holy to the Moros, apparently far more holy than it is to Americans, as the Moros are absolutely unyielding in their refusal to trade their holy rights for political convenience. They continue to fight to this day.

One of the things we learned in the 1902–1913 war with the Moros was that revolvers chambered in .38 Long Colt, with ballistic performance in the same class as today's .38 Special and 9x19mm Parabellum, were inadequate at stopping such a determined enemy. So were the army's 30-40 Krags, with performance almost indistinguishable from today's .308 Winchester or 7.62x51mm NATO. Many were the soldiers in that conflict who would have given anything for the trusty old big-bore 45-70, which the Krag had replaced. Many are the American soldiers today who must wonder in amazement that they are once again fighting Islamic militants with guns in the .38 Long Colt and 30-40 Krag class, or with so-called assault rifles that a Moro might find marginally useful for piercing his ears.

### 1906

Based on the ongoing clashes with the Moros, the U.S. Army came to the painful conclusion that a new military handgun was called for. Extensive ballistic testing on live cattle and human cadavers performed in 1904 (the famous Thompson-LaGarde tests), plus the cavalry's traditional requirement to shoot horses in battle as well as men, led to the determination by an army ordnance board headed by Col. John T. Thompson and Colonel LaGarde that the army needed a 45-caliber handgun to provide adequate stopping power. The selection process started in 1906 with firearms submitted by Colt, DWM/Luger, Savage, Smith & Wesson (S&W), Knoble, Bergmann, Webley-Scott, and White-Merrill.

John Browning, who was working for Colt at the time, had already developed a semiautomatic pistol around his .38 Colt Automatic cartridge (almost identical in performance to the 9mm, later improved in the .38 Super) that he knew he could reengineer to accommodate a more effective 45-caliber cartridge of his own design.

Browning's new pistol worked in an entirely different way than the paragons of semiautomatic pistols at the time—the Model 1896 broomhandle Mauser and the 1902 Luger, which was Georg Luger's improvement of the German-manufactured pistol designed by American Hugo Borchardt in 1893.

Browning's pistol was a radical, yet simple, recoil-operated, locked-breech, tilting barrel design. The barrel, slide, magazine, and frame were separate components. The barrel was attached to the frame by means of pins, which passed through pivoting links. The slide was fitted into channels in the frame. Ridges and grooves were machined into the top of the barrel at the chamber to match ridges and grooves on the inside of the slide. With the action closed, these ridges and grooves interlocked, the slide covered virtually the entire barrel, and the firing pin housing closed off the chamber. Lock-up was complete. Upon firing, recoil forced the slide and barrel to travel rearward together for about a quarter inch. The links caused the barrel to pivot downward at the same time, freeing the slide and barrel from their interlocking grooves. The slide then continued rearward to full recoil, extracting and ejecting the spent cartridge case and recocking the hammer. With the slide at full travel and the recoil spring fully compressed, the spring then took over and pushed the slide closed again as it stripped a fresh cartridge from the magazine and loaded it into the chamber. The operation of almost every semiautomatic pistol manufactured since has been based directly on this break-through design.

Browning and Colt had developed the new .45 ACP (Automatic Colt Pistol) cartridge in 1905, chambering it in a scaled-up pistol they called the Model 1905. The new .45 ACP round was loaded with a 230-grain FMJ (full metal jacket) bullet and matched the performance requirements the Moro-weary army officers were looking for. It was a further improved model of this pistol that Colt entered in the 1906 trials.

Only Colt and Savage survived those first trials. The ordnance department called for a series of further tests and experiments and appointed a final selection committee in 1911.

### 1911

The official birthday—March 29, 1911. After the most exhaustive test regimen in history, including subjecting the pistol to war-environment abuse and firing 6,000 rounds through it without a single jam or failure, the U.S. Army adopted the Automatic Pistol, Caliber .45, Model of 1911 as its official sidearm. The navy and marines quickly followed. Increased production capacity was set up at the government's Springfield Armory to meet the demand.

We've called that pistol the 1911 ever since. Colt simply calls it the O-frame. It has earned many more names over the years, some less than flattering.

### 1917

When Gavrilo Princip used one of Browning's little 7.65x17mm (.32 ACP) Model 1900 FN pistols to shoot the Archduke Francis Ferdinand of Austria in 1914, World War I was not long in coming. But it was Browning's big .45 auto that entered World War I on the hips of American amateur and professional soldiers alike, privates and generals, and everyone in between. It was estimated that 2.7 million pistols would be required for the war effort, and contracts were let out to several manufacturers besides Colt and Springfield Armory to meet the demand, including Remington/UMC, Winchester, Burroughs Adding Machine Co., Lanston Monotype Machine Co., National Cash Register Co., A.J. Savage Munitions Co., Savage Arms Co., and two Canadian firms, with Remington/UMC actually going into production and turning out about 22,000 pistols before the war's end.

More than 8 million soldiers and 13 million civilians were killed in that war. There are no records of how many lives were saved by the GI .45 automatic. We do know that a soldier by the name of Alvin York personally used his to save quite a few of ours by taking quite a few of theirs.

York was a corporal from Tennessee, the same state in which John Browning's father was born. When his patrol came under heavy machine gun fire on an October morning in 1918, resulting in its being pinned down and its leader killed along with several other American soldiers, York took command and started plinking enemy soldiers between the eyes with his Enfield M1917 as they popped their heads over the tops of their Maxim

machine guns. When York's rifle ran dry, the enemy patrol rushed him with bayonets from close range. That's when York's .45 automatic came into play, devastating the charging patrol and stopping it in its tracks. Continuing to fire his pistol and advance, York single-handedly killed 25 and captured 132 of the enemy. He was promoted to sergeant and awarded the French *Croix de Guerre* and the Congressional Medal of Honor. Few enemy soldiers ever underestimated the capabilities of a GI armed with a .45 auto again.

The heroic exploits of Sergeant York and others earned the big handgun widespread affection from the American public, who universally adopted the military's description of Colt's semiauto as the .45 automatic, though this name is more accurately applied to the Thompson submachine gun, which John T. Thompson of the aforementioned army ordnance board was quick to design around Browning's .45 ACP cartridge. The full-automatic Thompson was first publicly demonstrated in 1920, was an immediate hit, and was widely used by American civilians, the Irish Republican Army (IRA), the U.S. Post Office, the U.S. Marines, and the FBI, which issued Thompsons to its field offices until 1974.

Hollywood hack writers placed a tommy gun in the hands of every '30s-era gangster, real or invented. But it was a .45 automatic pistol that Machine Gun Kelly was armed with during his last standoff with the Memphis Police. It was a .45 automatic that John Dillinger kept under his pillow at night. It was an unfired .45 automatic that was found in Bonnie Parker's lap (and an unfired sawed-off 10-gauge shotgun that was found in Clyde Barrow's hand) when their bullet-riddled bodies were pulled from what was left of their car. And it was a brace of unfired .45 automatics that went down with Pretty Boy Floyd.

The .45 automatic is, of course, actually a .45 semiautomatic. A lot of full-auto conversions of the 1911 were made, and Star of Spain went into production with its fine 1911-pattern MD/PD machine pistols. Serious developmental work in the full-auto area was being done in this country up until 1934, when Franklin Roosevelt defied the U.S. Constitution and everything this country previously stood for with his National Firearms Act. At that time, the $200 federal tax attached to all automatic weapons transfers was the equivalent of about 10 weeks of wages for a working man, something like $10,000 today. The penalty for not paying the $200 tax was 10 years in prison, the equivalent of 10 years in prison even today.

At any rate, a one-hand weapon that fires big-bore bullets as fast as you can pull the trigger is hard to beat. However, as Bonnie Parker, Pretty Boy Floyd, and others found out, you do have to have the opportunity to pull the trigger.

### 1941

By the time World War II came around, the Model 1911 had become the Model 1911A1. It seems that, despite the government .45's well-earned reputation for ruggedness, reliability, and effectiveness, quite a few soldiers had come back from the Great War complaining that it kicked too much, was difficult to control, and they couldn't hit anything with it. Sgt. Alvin York was not among those whining.

The new 1911A1 featured crescent-shaped relief cuts machined into the frame around the trigger, an arched and checkered mainspring housing to replace the original flat one, a modified hammer spur, a short trigger with checkered face, an extended grip safety tang, and widened front and rear sights. These minor modifications, which may or may not have been improvements, were almost all accomplished by simply interchanging parts. Hybrids are therefore not unknown, some of which are quite collectible.

Some 2.5 million .45s were manufactured between 1941 and 1945, about half by subcontractors Remington-Rand, Ithaca, Union Switch and Signal Co., and the Singer Sewing Machine Company. Many of our allies used the 1911, and a number of foreign companies and governments were licensed to produce them. About 1,000 1911s were manufactured with Nazi markings when the Germans captured the licensed government arsenal in Norway and ordered production to start up again under their supervision.

And there were Sergeant Yorks in this war too.

In 1942, in the middle of the muddy midnight jungle of Guadalcanal, with a machine gun in one hand and a 1911 in the other, Marine G. Sgt. John Basilone single-handedly stopped a screaming banzai attack and completely wiped out a company of almost 100 Japanese trying to overrun his position. He became the second marine to be awarded the Medal of Honor in World War II.

Second Lt. Owen J. Baggett of the Tenth Air Force in India jumped out of his burning B-24 and, while floating slowly but not helplessly down in his parachute, came under attack by a Japanese Zero. Baggett quickly dispatched the enemy fighter plane by placing a 45-caliber, 230-grain bullet into the pilot's head.

Sr. Lt. Walt Hagan, a navy bomber pilot, was camped at a remote airstrip in the Philippines with a half dozen other aviators when they were attacked by native headhunters. Solid chest hits from the little 30-caliber M1 carbine wielded by one of the aviators failed to get anybody's attention, but Hagan's .45 quickly ended any biology lesson the worked-up savages may have had in mind. Shortly afterward, quite a few M1 carbines were traded for .45 automatics.

When Maj. "Dutch" van Kirk navigated his B-29 *Enola Gay* into the airspace above Hiroshima to deliver a 9,000-pound atomic bomb called Little Boy, he was carrying a World War I-era Colt 1911 on his belt. Just in case.

With the end of the Second World War, the government stopped buying 1911s and didn't buy another one for 40 years. On the commercial side, the 1911 market was booming. Colt developed the shorter, lighter-weight Commander on the first aluminum-alloy frame around 1949, the steel-framed Combat Commander in 1970, and the still smaller Officer's ACP about 1985. Other serious manufacturers with ambitious ideas—and often better quality control than union-plagued Colt—were joining the 1911 competition on a regular basis.

Despite the ready availability of new 1911s, Korea and Vietnam were fought with government surplus .45s, or .45s cobbled together with surplus parts. These 1911s were sidearms to a succession of ever less effective military rifles, from the 30-06 to the .308 to the .223. In the 1980s the army looked around and decided it needed a less powerful handgun as a more appropriate companion to its less powerful rifles. At about the same time, special operations looked around and decided that what it needed was some new 45-caliber 1911s that were more than a mismatched collection of leftover World War II parts. So, in keeping with the psychotic nature of its bureaucratic self, the government was rubbing the foreign political bellies of its little 9mm allies with its left hand at the same time it was buying .45 ACP 1911s again with its right.

### 1957

In the summer of 1957, U.S. Marine Corps Lt. Col. Jeff Cooper, looking very much like he had just stepped up to the line in one of the more extravagant of today's Cowboy Action Shooting matches, made a fast draw from leather and pulled the trigger on a Colt Model 1911 .45 ACP. It was the First Annual Leatherslap he had organized at Big Bear Lake in California. And nothing would ever be the same again.

During World War II Cooper first spent 30 months as a marine officer attached to the battleship USS *Pennsylvania*. He was then assigned to Camp Pendleton to teach less experienced marine officers how to train their people to wage war, and from there to the Command and Staff School at Quantico, where he was an instructor in military intelligence and where, incidentally, he took the time to demonstrate to his FBI neighbors the superiority of the 1911 semiautomatic pistol over 38-caliber revolvers (though it would take a few more decades for that lesson to sink into the bureaucratic brains of the bureau). It was at Quantico that Cooper and another distinguished marine pistol shot, then Capt. Howie Taft, worked together on 1911 techniques and tactics to develop the Advanced Practical Pistol Course adopted by the Pentagon, thus planting the roots of revolution.

Cooper was back in the saddle during the Korean War, a bloody conflict almost as forgotten as the Moro wars in the Philippines. This war, which was not called a war, resulted in the deaths of a million of our South Korean allies, more than half a million Chinese Communists, a million North Korean Communists, both military and civilian, and 54,000 Americans. Cooper's work in Korea was with the intelligence community, and it is a subject he does not discuss, though his daughter Lindy has written that he spent a great deal of time in the remote up-country, as well as in Washington, D.C., on Saipan, and in Bangkok; learned to fly a DC-3; and demonstrated to his very personal satisfaction the lethal effects of .45 ACP hardball injected into vital organs of the enemy at close range. Returned to almost-civilian life, Cooper taught firearms handling, mental conditioning, and personal protection to private groups and governments all over the world. He taught race-car driving with Dan Gurney. And he taught history at the University of California until the repulsive little world of academia turned his head to more pleasant pursuits.

Cooper organized the First Annual Leatherslap as a quick-draw contest among friends. It soon grew into the Bear Valley Gunslingers, which competed on a regular basis, acted as the proving ground for Cooper's growing combat shooting doctrine, and finally expanded into the Southwest Combat Pistol League. (The California secretary of state insisted that they delete the word "combat" from their name.) The Modern Technique of the Pistol grew out of this experience and would soon give birth to the International Practical Shooting Confederation (IPSC) and to the American Pistol Institute at Cooper's Gunsite Ranch in Arizona, the premier firearms training center in the world. Military, police, and civilian use of the pistol would change forever.

All the gun-ignorant draftees who escaped back into civilian life after the wars braying that the .45 kicked too hard and they couldn't hit anything with it were suddenly shut up. Cooper was proving that, for any man capable of learning fundamental skills, the 1911 was the best way to conclude a gunfight. And he was fully qualified and prepared to teach serious handgunners exactly how to do it. The Modern Technique of the Pistol took full advantage, for the first time, of the ultramodern capabilities that had been inherent in the design of the 1911 from the beginning. After half a century of frontline soldiering, the 1911 shifted into second gear.

In a recent discussion, Cooper told me, in his typically understated fashion, "I thought that target shooting was impractical. I got some people interested and we started making things closer to reality, insofar as we could. We tried to make measures and tests that would be more relevant to the way the pistol is used."

Cooper was the guiding light of the revolution, but he was not alone. "I worked with and shot with all the old masters," he said. "The guy who invented the Weaver stance was Jack Weaver. I would say that Ray Chapman was the master stylist; he was the best technical practitioner. Elden Carl was probably the best performer in terms of measured technique. Thell Reed, of course, was the speed burner. And John Plahn was a theorizer, he was a doctor in physical education, and he took the systems that we used to shoot with and evaluated them so that they could be taught. The teacher must first of all know *why*. That's something we studied hard, but we didn't really know why we were doing what we were doing until John Plahn analyzed it with photography."

Highly developed physical technique based on the universal platform of John Browning's 1911 pistol was one component of the Cooper doctrine. The most important component, however, was mental. "Mind-set is everything," he said, as he looked hard into my eyes. "A willingness to take the step."

1957 was not only the acknowledged start date of the combat pistolcraft revolution, it was also the year the first American soldier died in combat in Vietnam—though our involvement in that war, which was not called a war, would not be officially recognized for another six years.

## 1967

Along about the mid-1960s, when American soldiers were doing their very best to fight born-again Communists in the jungles and tunnels in and around Vietnam despite stateside commanders who were only concerned with

rolling around in bed with the whores of politics, domestic law enforcement found itself on a wartime footing as well. The intellectually corrupt academic community discovered that it could manipulate the glandular spasms of overmothered children—roving in undisciplined packs over college and high school campuses and through drug-rotten inner city cores nationwide—and send them out into the streets to achieve alien academia's treacherous and traitorous goals.

Following the self-destructive Watts riots in the black ghetto of south-central L.A., the Los Angeles Police Department (LAPD) formed and trained a special unit to deal more efficiently in a combat-zone environment. The first element of this unit was in place by 1967 and was called the Special Weapons And Tactics team. Better known by its acronym, SWAT, this new commando-type unit would influence law enforcement thinking around the world. Along with the most advanced tactical rifles, shotguns, and automatic weapons ever invented, the pistol of choice was the big-bore, single-action 1911.

Most cops, like most other people, watch too many cop-as-social-worker shows on TV and are burdened with a politically correct abhorrence of killing people who richly deserve it. As a result, most cops know as much about guns as the thimble-collecting wife of the catch-and-release fly fisherman who lives down the street.

On the other hand, cops who make it or even try their best to make it on their department's SWAT team are a different breed. They are likely to be warrior types with a thirst for high-speed training, and they tend to know their guns. You should not be surprised at the overwhelming number of 45-caliber 1911s you find in the holsters of local and federal SWAT, HRT (Hostage Rescue Team), and other highly trained law enforcement units today.

## 1976

In May 1976, 40 top shooters from around the world gathered in Columbia, Missouri, to attend the International Pistol Conference under the chairmanship of Lt. Col. Jeff Cooper. The conference officially founded IPSC and charted the course of defensive handgun marksmanship for decades to come. Cooper was acclaimed first IPSC world president; a constitution was established; and the keystone combat shooting components of accuracy, power, and speed were translated into the Latin motto, *Diligentia, Vis, Celeritas*.

Almost immediately, IPSC and the combat shooting competitions it sponsored took off in a big way, spreading all over the civilized world, reinvigorating the civilian 1911 market, creating a nationwide cottage industry of competition parts manufacturers, and dominating the configuration of 1911 pistols for a very vigorous 20 years. The 1911 had gone to the races, and no other pistol could hope to compete against it.

As I recall, one of the most refreshing of the original IPSC bylaws was the pledge that only those countries would be allowed to compete who permitted their citizens to freely own firearms and

use them in self-defense. The first IPSC World Championship was held in Austria, a country whose shooters are currently engaged in a life-and-death struggle with their government over restrictive gun laws. The second IPSC World Championship was held in Rhodesia (today's Zimbabwe), and the third championship was held in South Africa. Australians are allowed to compete in international IPSC matches even though they willingly gave up their gun rights years ago. British shooters are still allowed to compete even though they are now compelled by their socialist governments to store their guns offshore and leave the so-called United Kingdom even to practice.

I wonder what Winston Churchill and T.E. Lawrence, both of whom traded in their broomhandle Mausers for Colt 1911s at the earliest opportunity, would have to say about the

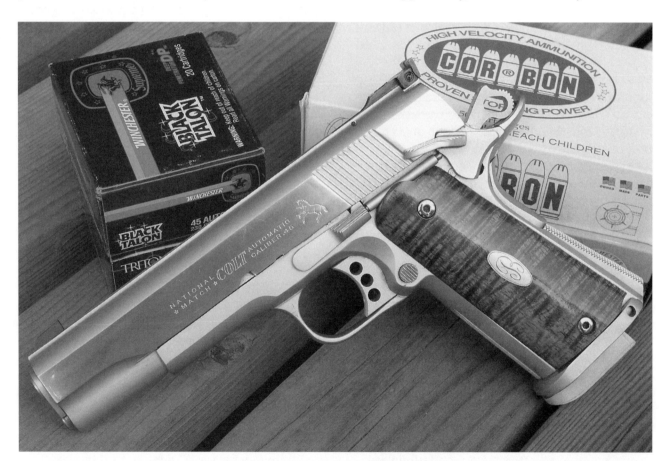

One of the author's very personal 1911s is his customized Colt National Match. The 50-year-old gun has seen stiff IPSC competition, been carried on a daily basis, done its duty to protect a few national political figures, and even delivered some game to the pot. Photo by Morgan W. Boatman.

forced disarming of all British subjects. The British Labour Party has succeeded in achieving a goal much desired for the British by Adolf Hitler, his failure due in large part to our delivering into the hands of the unprepared Brits many thousands of 1911s and every other gun we could spare at the time. It is not known whether Churchill ever actually fired his 1911, but there is plenty of evidence that Lawrence of Arabia used his quite often and very well.

Even in the United States today, competition is limited to those handgun models and configurations grudgingly left off the prohibited list drawn up by the democratically elected idiot politicians of our time. Some American IPSC competitors buy pistols from Canadian companies who aren't even allowed to sell their guns to their own citizens. So much for the lip service paid to political freedom at Columbia, Missouri, in 1976.

The forces that eventually ruptured IPSC, however, came not so much from external evil as from internal schoolboyishness. As in any group of males, two hostile camps soon established themselves. The martial artists camp viewed IPSC competition as a high-pressure way to ingrain effective combat habits in preparation for deadly-force encounters in real life. For the opposing camp, IPSC was just a game, not very different from pinball or golf, and the only point of playing it was to win it, through rule-juggling, regulation-weaseling, outright cheating if you could get away with it, constant complaining and whining and, of course, never-ending equipment races.

To the undoubted surprise of the game-players, the electronic sighting systems, recoil compensators, extended magazines, rail-mounted accessories, and even some of the exaggerated controls common on highly impractical open-class IPSC guns exerted a profound influence on certain specialized units of the military. Some of the offensive, assault-oriented 1911s built for the Navy SEALs, the Army's Delta Force, and Marine Force Recon bear a striking resemblance to the raceguns developed for all-out IPSC competition.

The martial artists, meanwhile, went off and formed a new organization called the International Defensive Pistol Association (IDPA)

to better concentrate on the tactical deployment of their 1911s and other pistols in the defensive role best suited to civilians, law enforcement personnel, and everybody else other than well-organized military ambush teams. It is IDPA that is influencing the new generation of fighting 1911s being built by gunsmiths and factories today. But you can already see the camp boundaries reforming among IDPA's escalating number of shooters. Boys will be boys.

The present culture of IPSC can be inferred from recent comments of the current president: "Although the roots are martial in origin, the sport matured from these beginnings . . . Now, IPSC shooting is an international sport, emphasizing safety and safe gun handling. The crowning glory for practical shooting is to become the IPSC World Champion." Sounds much like pole-vaulting. The president does admit, apparently with some chagrin, that "in fact, some matches even contain surprise stages where no one knows in advance what to expect."

I recall Cooper telling me once, "Nobody ever said, 'I'm alive today because I'm an excellent shot.' They say, 'I'm alive today because I learned how to think.'" The closest Jeff Cooper has ever come to commenting directly on today's IPSC in my presence was during a fireside discussion of our mutual enjoyment of swordplay. A faraway look clouded the colonel's face as he said, "Fencing, of course, suffered the same fate as IPSC. The fencing foil is of no use at all in a fight."

## 1985

Progress being a strange phenomenon that moves backward as often as forward, in 1985 the 1911 pistol and .45 ACP cartridge were replaced as official U.S. military issue by the Italian-made Beretta Model 92 pistol firing the 9mm Parabellum cartridge. The Beretta is a large pistol of complicated double-action/single-action design holding multiple rounds of a small European cartridge. The little 9x19mm cartridge was introduced in 1902 for the Luger pistol, which was first adopted as an ornamental sidearm worn by the German navy in 1904.

The 9mm was widely carried but seldom

used by the European armies of our enemies in World Wars I and II. When it was used, and when the pistol worked, the little cartridge quickly, and fortunately for our side, proved that it was not an effective man-stopper. We already knew that. As previously noted, the failure of small-bore pistols to influence the mind-set of determined adversaries was demonstrated on a rather large scale in the Philippines as early as 1902. Nevertheless, the obsolete 9mm was deemed a more appropriate companion piece to the small varmint rifle then in use by our armed forces. What the hell, the guns were rarely even loaded anyway.

The U.S. Marine Corps, exerting its recognized authority as the world's military small-arms experts, did not rush to give up its combat-proven 45-caliber 1911 pistols for the big new Beretta firing the little old 9mm cartridge. Nor did the better-trained special forces of other U.S. military branches. In every military conflict going on today anywhere in the world, among the elite soldiers who actually use their handguns along with the most sophisticated rifles and submachine guns available, the preferred handgun continues to be the 45-caliber 1911. A professional soldier knows the difference between a pistol and a staple gun.

Given the recently demonstrated questionable adequacy of the hypersensitive 9mm Beretta pistol to properly deal with a herd of religious fanatics stampeding through a sandstorm, which is the definitive portrait of our current enemy, the Pentagon has now let out contracts for the new manufacture of .45 ACP 1911s. Not a new design (that's been tried, and the dismal results have been tallied), just new manufacture of what has always worked. Even the deskbound generals of the new army are not stupid enough to cling to the bureaucratic dream of improving the shape of the wheel by committee decree.

## 1987

Something happened in 1987 that stood the country on its ear, revealed how American citizens really feel about their right to bear arms,

and wiped the noses of antigun politicians in their own excrement. Florida drafted the nation's most enlightened and thoroughgoing shall-issue .concealed-carry law, sparking a civilian carry movement that spread across the country like wildfire. All manner of 1911 pistols were showing up in more civilian holsters than ever before, Gunsite-like training academies sprouted like sunflowers, and handgun competition reoriented its priorities from the impractical "practical" guns of IPSC to the fighting "defensive" guns of IDPA almost overnight. The 1911 was returning to its roots.

There are those among us who consider a concealed-carry permit redundant, another unwelcome intrusion of the government into something that is none of its business, another tax-raising scheme demanding a license to exercise an inalienable right. We have always carried guns and don't care whether anybody approves of it or not. But after 1987, even timid, ordinary, law-abiding citizens were assured that they would not be prohibited from exercising the U.S. Constitution and that official paperwork would eventually be issued by some overpaid government clerk to prove it.

Today, the majority of Americans live in states where they can legally carry a concealed handgun if they want to. Predictably, most people don't want to. They have lost their taste for self-determination and are not prepared to accept such a lonely responsibility. We can assume that the few people of this type who were around circa 1776 stayed hidden beneath their beds or locked in their basements. Too many modern Americans have bought the cheap political idea that paying an excessive amount of taxes to an incompetent government will somehow protect them from any evil that may lurk in the shadows. After subverting the Constitution in order to shut down the Italian Mafia, the U.S. government now enjoys an uncontested monopoly on the old protection racket. And there has never been any shortage of naive victims.

Nevertheless, since 1987, street criminals have have become suddenly wary because they can no longer be entirely sure that their prey will always be as docile and helpless and cowardly as an Englishman, a Scot or an Irishman, a Canadian or an Australian, or the recent aberration of the castrated American. Only the most politically backward regions of the country—New York and Massachusetts; Maryland and Washington, D.C.; the cities of California; and some in the upper Midwest can still legally get away with treating American citizens like serfs and outlawing their right to defend themselves. As more and more states pass legislation honoring each other's concealed-carry permits, psychotic predators are being given a clear map of where they can safely go to receive keys to the city from the local mayor and practice their violent behavior with impunity. The map also clearly delineates those areas the violent criminal had better stay clear of lest he risk taking a .45 hollowpoint in the chest from a grandmother pushing a baby buggy.

We can thank the NRA for organizing the grassroots troops and leading the state-by-state legal battles. We can thank Jeff Cooper for enlightening the more wakeful among us to the high levels of personal competence possible with a little discipline and intelligent training. And we can thank John Browning for giving us something to put in our holsters that will get the job done.

## TODAY AND TOMORROW

Countless new semiautomatic pistols have been introduced during the life of the 1911, and every one that has survived to carve out a successful niche for itself owes its existence to the design fundamentals of John Browning's 1911. The Glock, which has made such an amazing impact on the handgun world with its unique trigger mechanism and high-tech polymer frame, would not have been able to fire a shot were it not for the recoil-operated tilting barrel design taken directly from Browning's 1911. Nor would the Glock have been so easily accepted by firearms trainers if, like the Beretta and other complicated double-action semiautomatics, its training regimen was significantly different from that of the single-action 1911.

Everything there is to say about the 1911 has surely already been said. It is undoubtedly the most written-about gun there ever was.

Rather amazingly, gun writers have even more to say about it today than at any time in its long past. If anything is missing from all this, perhaps it's perspective.

First and foremost, the 1911 is a fighting pistol, a supremely effective instrument of freedom and defense. There may be people, as I have heard, who believe in pounding their swords into plowshares, but I don't know any. I do know some people who would have given anything to be able to pound their plowshares into .45 automatics. And a few hundred million others who were forced to give up everything because they couldn't.

In the grotto warfare of Afghanistan and the street fighting in Iraq and whatever battles, skirmishes, struggles, confrontations, and shootouts are to come, the 1911 is as useful and crucial a tool as it ever has been. If not more so. At the height of the close-quarters cave-clearing operations in Afghanistan, the going price for a 1911 was three Berettas and a bottle of hooch. Gladly paid.

I received a message recently from a supervising special agent with the U.S. Department of State's Diplomatic Security Service stationed in a hot spot overseas. The man was a

It's kind of a shame to conceal a good-looking 1911 when you can show it off in something like this Holdridge rig from Kirkpatrick Leather. Photo by the author.

deeply experienced shooter, familiar with the 1911 since childhood. He had carried a 1911 in a professional capacity for other government agencies and won a number of law enforcement shooting matches with it. At one point in his career, he was asked to trade in his .45 for a 9mm Beretta M9, which he refers to as a "spaghetti Walther" and about which he had this to say: "The M9 is simply too fat for many hands, too big for its cartridge, and simply not powerful enough to get the job done, as the most recent conflicts our military has been involved in have shown. Even more importantly and sadly, inside of three years of those Berettas arriving I pulled no less than five off the rack that wouldn't go bang when the trigger was pulled. I couldn't begin to say what was wrong because, not having a Beretta armorer's tool kit handy, it's impossible to replace broken parts on the M9 without sending the piece up to depot-level maintenance."

Having survived the "spaghetti Walther" state of affairs, he now finds himself in an even more dangerous environment and saddled with a SIG. He writes,

Now here I am as an agent overseas forced to rely on the P228 in 9x19mm. The pistol itself is a fine little machine and interesting to play with. However, as a member of one of the smaller and more active federal law enforcement agencies in service I think it sad that those in a position to make such decisions have settled on something less than optimum for our uses both domestically and abroad. My main purpose in writing you is to get your thoughts on the best way to go about trying to initiate a change in the thinking of our equipment personnel regarding selection of our service handgun. I believe that the 1911 is just about the best sidearm we could use for our roles, far from other armed American support. I know there are many in my organization who agree with me but aren't willing to press the issue and make any waves.

There are women and even some men in DS whose hands are too small to be as effective marksmen with the SIG as they otherwise would be with a tool that was properly proportioned. It's unnerving on the range seeing both male and female agents having to completely shift that SIG around almost 90 degrees in their hands so they can reach and pull that first crunch. The potential for losing the piece in a real fight exists there. The 1911 is very well suited for hands of various sizes.

We . . . are in the unenviable position of being out of reach of any significant armed American assistance for a minimum of 24 hours realistically if the stuff hits the fan. And likely the only thing we'll have available is our service handgun, all long guns being secured in safes. As you can tell, this is an intensely personal matter to me, as fighting handguns are a strongly personal matter for anyone who takes their training and nature of their job seriously can attest. Happily, I have not had to shoot for blood but I have spoken with a number of colleagues and friends who have, and those who have used 9mm handguns have stated a lack of positive results despite excellent marksmanship while those who used large-bore handguns have achieved uniformly satisfactory results.

In this line of work as in other forms of law enforcement and military service there has to be a line drawn and certain things laid out right from the start regarding the best tool for any given job. I believe that the 1911 remains the single best hard-use sidearm suitable for common issue to any group of professionals who may actually have to depend on that sidearm for their lives or the protection of the lives of others around them.

This is not the kind of cry for help one ignores, and I pursued the issue with everyone I knew who might have something relevant to say about it, including politicians, intelligence officers, and weapons instructors. The consensus of opinion, including that of the agent involved, was that questionable equipment selection was merely a symptom of larger ailments at the State Department.

It is well known that the State Department has been the most hard-core nest of leftists in our government since the 1930s, and it has always resisted even the most earnest efforts to eradicate America's enemies within. Nothing has changed. Unfortunately for our inadequately armed agent, nothing is likely to change. One of the State Department-watchers I talked to said, "No State Department agent will ever be allowed to carry a 45-caliber 1911. Because, if he did, he might kill one of our enemies."

Personally, I've always thought of the 1911 as a very personal gun. A pistol to be proud of, better carried openly than concealed whenever possible, preferably in a holster of fine leather (though the new generation of Kydex is eminently sensible). A true sidearm. Personal and personalized. More than a racegun or last-ditch defense weapon or collector's piece, though it can be all of these as well. A pistol that's so comfortable and comforting to shoot that you shoot it frequently, every chance you get, at most anything you feel like shooting.

The millions of rounds that have come blasting out of the short barrel of John Browning's 1911 since its birth on the snowy slopes of the rugged mountains way out west have created countless adventure stories of their own all over the world. They have given birth to enduring legends, revealed universal truths, blown locked

A new generation of 1911 builders has no trouble following John Browning's hundred-year-old footprints. The talent of custom pistolsmith Kase Reeder of Flagstaff, Arizona, runs in the family. Photo by the author.

gates to freedom right off their hinges, and changed the course of history.

You were warned. This is only the beginning of a very long story.

# Not All 1911s Are .45s

## 1

Texas Ranger Joaquin Jackson spent his career with a 45-caliber Colt Government Model 1911 on his hip patrolling the harsh and isolated Big Bend country, a huge bulge in the state where, to this day, the most vital signs of life are rattlesnakes, mountain lions, and outlaws with a bigger and more poisonous bite than the first two combined, where in many places at certain times of the year the only water for more than a hundred miles is the muddy Rio Grande, called Rio Bravo by the Mexicans on the other side and still the most dangerous international border in the world. Somebody once asked Jackson why he carried a Colt .45. He replied, "Because they don't make a Colt .46."

Well, Joaquin, they make damn near everything else.

## A LITTLE TIME TRAVEL: THE .38 SUPER

In 1929, an audacious new chambering was introduced in the 1911 pistol. This was the first time the big semiauto was available in any caliber other than .45 ACP, and it was one of the first steps into the coming era of high-velocity, high-pressure cartridges. The round was the .38 Super. It was the .357 Magnum of its time, promoted as the most powerful auto pistol cartridge in the world. Even today, it is one of the dominant calibers in IPSC competition, where the 1911 continues to reign and a certain power factor beyond the practical limits of the 9mm Parabellum must be reached in order to play the game effectively.

The fact is, the .38 Super is nothing more than a hot-loaded .38 Colt Automatic, a cartridge John Browning designed in 1900. Pushing little 125-grain 9mm bullets in

Springfield Armory has captured the quintessential character of an emblematic sidearm in this elegant production of its .38 Super 1911A1. Flat-shooting and accurate, the classic Springfield Armory rendition features highly polished chrome plating and dazzling mother-of-pearl grips on the traditional 1911A1 frame. The synthetic pearl grips function as well as the authentic kind in their practical application of preventing the grip from slipping in even a sweaty palm, which is the reason pearl grips were used so often on early target pistols. It is also comforting to see a hammer that looks like a hammer. Despite the protestations of ham-handed gun writers, the spur hammer, even with the original grip safety, does not bite the web of most hands. It never did. Beavertail grip safeties with Commander-style hammers were not invented to solve this rare problem, but to provide a higher grip. This big, flashy Springfield is a pistol of simple, if not exactly quiet, dignity. Photo by Morgan W. Boatman.

the neighborhood of 1,200–1,250 feet per second (fps) in factory loads, the .38 Super is flat-shooting, accurate, and indeed capable of churning out a few more foot-pounds of kinetic energy than most factory-loaded .45 ACPs, though even in those days (or, rather, especially in those days) it was widely recognized that kinetic energy is not the crucial factor in stopping power.

The .38 Super is a semirimmed cartridge originally designed to headspace on its very small rim. Since the late 1980s, however, manufacturers have chambered their pistols to headspace the .38 Super on its case mouth instead, like most other auto pistol cartridges, and a vast improvement over its previously so-so accuracy has been the result. Because the .38 Super has a case length 0.14 inch longer than the 9mm Parabellum, combat shooting competitors discovered that they could hand-

load it as hot as they wished without greatly exceeding IPSC-legal chamber pressure and make "major" caliber in a gun that not only has considerably less recoil than a .45 but also operates a compensator more effectively because of its higher pressure.

The most important legacy of the .38 Super, however, is not on the competition course but on the streets of Latin American cities. Because of bizarre laws against civilian ownership of military-caliber weapons like the .45 ACP south of the border, the .38 Super has long been the classical Latin version of the 1911. There is plenty of anecdotal evidence to suggest that the .38 Super cartridge, folded into the ultra-efficient 1911 design, has sufficed in its self-protection role quite nicely and has saved many individual lives throughout Mexico, Central America, and South America over the years.

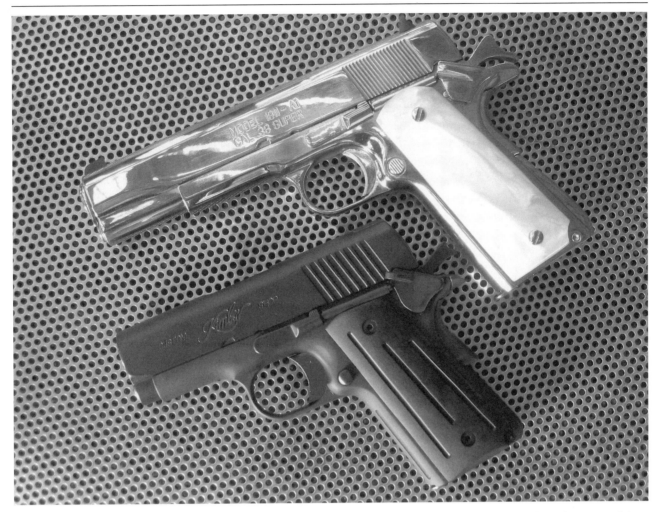

The Springfield Armory 1911A1 in .38 Super (above) is a traditional gun in an often-underrated caliber. Kimber RCP II (below) is a state-of-the-art 1911 in the traditional, original, and still unbeatable .45 ACP caliber. Photo by the author.

## WHY, WHY, WHY: THE 9MM PARABELLUM

There are only three reasons I can think of why anybody would want a 1911 chambered in 9x19mm Parabellum: (1) he has dozens of buckets of surplus 9mm ammo he doesn't know what to do with and figures the 1911 is the only pistol that won't come apart before the buckets are all gone; (2) his visiting brother-in-law works for NATO and he would like to make him feel at home but can't bring himself to buy a Beretta; (3) he is recoil-phobic to a neurotic degree, never kills anything more substantial than an aluminum beer can, and, on top of that, simply doesn't know any better.

A 2 1/2-pound 1911 is too much gun for the little 9mm Parabellum cartridge, an early offspring

of the .30 Luger, which has about the same power as the .38 Colt Automatic of 1900 vintage. The recoil impulse is so light as to be nonexistent, and you may find yourself staring down the barrel to see if anything came out when you pulled the trigger. If you're a committed student of the small-fast-bullet school, you're better off with a .38 Super, which is a 9mm that is, at least, fast.

Another message I recently received from another frustrated law enforcement agent:

A couple weeks ago, an agent assigned to my old field office in New York was involved in a shooting incident I thought you may find informative. The agent was entering an apartment building in New York City to visit his mother when he was immediately confronted by a man armed with a .38 revolver who demanded his wallet. He complied, taking his wallet out of his pocket and tossing it to the floor between him and the goblin. For whatever reason, the goblin—who, it turned out, has a long rap sheet that includes a previous manslaughter conviction—got very angry and decided to advance on the agent. At this point the agent simultaneously began moving for whatever cover was near, drew his department-issued SIG 228 loaded with 14 rounds of 124-grain 9mm Hydra-Shok, and ordered the goblin to drop his revolver. Then the shots were fired.

I don't know who fired the first round, but the goblin fired one round, apparently very near the agent's head as he had powder burns and bullet splatter on his face. The agent fired 14 rounds, scoring 11 hits, one or two of which removed the assailant's testicles. None of the shots proved fatal. After [the agent got] behind cover and continued to shout orders for the goblin to drop the revolver, the goblin stood there, gun in hand, for several seconds before [he said] that he felt tired, dropped the revolver, and sat on the floor. Last I heard the goblin was still in the hospital but alive. Our agent was cleared of any wrongdoing, although I've not heard if NY is going to try to throw him in jail for having the audacity to defend himself against someone who was going to kill him.

This is yet another in a very long list of failures of the 9mm Parabellum to properly perform the task of any defensive handgun cartridge. I've written yet again to a fellow agent on the firearms policy review board regarding the issue of our duty cartridge and am also preparing a position paper I intend to submit making the case for switching to the .45 ACP and at least allowing agents the option of obtaining a 1911-pattern duty pistol.

I just wanted to let you know about this incident of a government agency inflicting the wrong tools for a job on its employees. Hope all is well with you in the land of the free.

### NEW LAW ENFORCEMENT STANDARD: THE STAR-QUALITY .40

The father of the .40 was the powerful 10mm. The mother was a lady FBI agent who managed to get off one round of 10mm before she broke down in tears. The midwife was the FBI armorer in the back room who pointed out to someone in charge that the big, new 10mm S&Ws were committing suicide in alarming numbers by cracking their frames. Thus the .40 was born, a 10mm with its brass abbreviated for more efficient burning of the lighter powder charge that seemed to make everybody happy.

The .40 (.40 Auto, .40 S&W, 10mm Short; call it what you will) is, in fact, an excellent compromise between the small-fast-bullet and the big-slow-bullet schools of thought, in that it moves bullets of reasonable weight at reasonably fast velocities. It is certainly a major improvement in performance over the 9mm, with the added advantage that the cartridge is compact enough to fit into a 9mm-size frame. Actually, the fact that the .40 does not require the larger frame that the .45 and 10mm must have is more than an extra advantage; it's the reason the .40 seized the law enforcement market almost overnight. Who could turn down a big boost over 9mm performance free of the charge of added weight and size? The cops couldn't, and neither could civilians.

If the .40 made the 9mm obsolete in all quarters save NATO and L.A. street gangs, its smashing success was less than impressive to fans of the 1911. They already had a gun big enough to handle a .45, so why would they want to chamber a smaller round?

### HOT! THE 10MM

If the 1911 is too much gun for the 9mm and the .40, the full-power 10mm is too much cartridge for the 1911. S&W frames weren't the only ones cracked by this founder of the new school of the big, fast bullet.

The 10mm cartridge was essentially the brainchild of Jeff Cooper and first saw the light of day in 1984 in the reworked CZ-75 "Bren Ten" pistols manufactured by Dornaus & Dixon Enterprises. The Bren Ten was positioned as the natural heir to the .45 ACP and could deliver .41 Magnum-level performance to back up its claim. The gun made its public debut in the hands of Detective Sonny Crocket on the popular television show *Miami Vice,* despite which, and in all seriousness, it was and is a truly great cartridge. Dornaus & Dixon, however, were better at marketing than financial management, and a series of money mistakes (and cracked frames) drove the company under.

Norma Ammunition, in the meantime, had gone into full production of 10mm auto ammo. And the S&W 1006, Colt Delta Elite, and Springfield Armory Omega were soon available to handle the hot new round—or, rather, handle it as long as they could before their frames started cracking and their parts started falling off. Norma's loading for the 10mm was a 200-grain bullet driven at an honest 1,200 fps, and it was a slide-battering pistol-breaker. Not even the beefed-up Springfield frames could stand up to such a cartridge for long.

And that's why the FBI's "Lite" 10mm load, which was translated into the standard .40 load, is mostly what you'll find masquerading as 10mm ammo from the big factories today. A number of smaller companies, notably Cor-Bon, Georgia Arms, and Texas Ammunition Co., go out of their way to make legitimate full-power 10mm ammo that meets or exceeds Norma's original loading. They don't make it for lady FBI agents; they make it for guys who take their pressure and velocity straight up, shaken not stirred.

A word of advice: if you want a 10mm auto and you intend to feed it a steady diet of full-power loads, get a Glock. The flexible polymer frame fights back when faced with abuse, and the fact that Glock designed the G20 and G29 for the 10mm in the first place means you probably won't be in for any unpleasant surprises.

## NAME YOUR CALIBER: .22 to .50

You can get a .22 Long Rifle conversion kit for your 1911 and shoot practically for free. The kits include a replacement slide, barrel, magazine, guide rod, and return spring; several companies make them; and they're remarkably quick, easy, accurate, and reliable. Some other caliber conversions are as simple, some more so, some not.

You can find 1911s chambered for .30 Luger, .41 Action Express, 9x21mm, 9x25 Dillon, .357 SIG, .38 Special Wadcutter, .224 Boz, 38-45, .38 Casull, .41 Avenger, .400 Cor Bon, .450 SMC, .40 Super, .45 Super, .460 Rowland, .451 Detonics, and I'm sure I've forgotten a few that are probably better forgotten. Some of these calibers are or have been available from the factory; many are simple conversions. Others, like the .357 Magnum Coonan and the stretched .45 Winchester Magnum Grizzly, were built on proprietary frames. Gary Reeder, the well-known custom pistolsmith in Flagstaff, Arizona, is threatening to build a scaled-up 1911 frame to accommodate a 50-caliber hunting cartridge of his own design.

Between you and your favorite gunsmith, you can probably have a 1911 in 5.5mm Velo Dog if you want one. But do you truly want one?

Left to right: 10mm, a great cartridge but a little too hot for a standard 1911 frame to handle; .45 ACP, the cartridge that defines the 1911 pistol and vice versa, a marriage made in handgun heaven; .40 Auto, the shortened and downloaded 10mm that now rules the world of U.S. law enforcement; .38 Super, what the little 9mm Parabellum would like to be if it could grow up.

## ARE YOU SURE YOU
## DON'T WANT A .45 ACP?

The 1911 pistol and the .45 ACP cartridge were born in the same bed, produced out of the same focused mind more or less undamaged by outside distractions. They've been together going on a hundred years and are as compatible and elegant a couple as you could ever hope to meet. Their respective sizes, shapes, weights, and moves complement each other. They tango very well together. (Did you know that Jeff and Janelle Cooper were contest-winning tango dancers in their misspent youths?) You would have to be some kind of monster to want to separate the two at this stage, although it appears to be a still-early stage with no sign of decrepit age anywhere in sight.

It was 1901 when Teddy Roosevelt appointed Brig. Gen. William Crozier as chief of army ordnance. And it was Crozier who, in 1904, assigned Capt. John T. Thompson of the infantry and Maj. Louis Anatole LaGarde of the medical corps to investigate and recommend which caliber should be used in a new service handgun. Thompson and LaGarde quickly rustled up a small herd of live beef cattle, unsuspecting deer, and naked human cadavers and headed for the Nelson Morris Company Union Stockyards in Chicago with as many different types of handguns, calibers, and bullet designs as they could lay their hands on—from the 7.65 (.30) Luger and .38 ACP to the .455 "Man-Stopper" and the .476 Eley, with lead roundnose, FMJ, flatpoint, and hollowpoint (19th century hollowpoint) bullets. It was these tests that resulted in the adoption of the .45 ACP (the actual diameter of the bullet is .452") as the official U.S. Army handgun cartridge.

On the first day in the slaughterhouse, Thompson and LaGarde simply shot the live animals a few times and clocked how long it took each one to die. With the smaller calibers, the gun often ran dry without anything much happening, and the two researchers had to beat the bovines to death by hammering them over the head (using a proper hammer, not the butts of their guns). Of course, they meticulously documented how many hammer blows were required to finish them off. In general, this methodology got to be messy, so for the second day of testing they decided to shoot the animals rapid-fire until either they fell down or 10 shots were fired.

During the human cadaver testing, the bodies were hung up by their heads so they could swing freely when hit by a bullet. They were shot from distances ranging from 9 feet to 75 yards, targeting both fleshy areas and bones. When a round struck a fleshy area, there was minimum sway. When a round struck a bone, the body moved enough so that Thompson and LaGarde could assign a number value to the observed swing for comparison purposes.

This whole exercise must have been a lot of fun for the two army academics, but it really didn't prove a damn thing. Using the same kind of scientific methodology today's academics use to come up with phenomena like global warming and secondhand smoke, Thompson and LaGarde built a case for the premise they had arrived at before descending on the stockyards of Chicago. And that's why the debate over "the best man-stopping cartridge" continues to rage. When Thompson and LaGarde concluded that the .45 was the most effective cartridge for a handgun they got lucky, because history has pretty much confirmed that their instincts were not incorrect.

They wrote in their report, "The Board was of the opinion that a bullet, which will have the shock effect and stopping effect at short ranges necessary for a military pistol or revolver, should have a caliber not less than .45." But then they added a disclaimer, which is of more true and lasting value than probably any other insight either of them had for the remainders of their military careers. They wrote, "Soldiers armed with pistols or revolvers should be drilled unremittingly in the accuracy of fire" because most of the human body offers "no hope of stopping an adversary by shock or other immediate results when hit."

At any rate, Browning's response was a 230-grain jacketed bullet with a muzzle velocity of 830 fps. And it offered more hope than most.

Without opening that whole Sanow-Marshall-Fackler nest of stopping-power claims, counterclaims, and scientific and not-so-scientific methodologies, I would like to quote a 30-year law enforcement veteran and trainer by the name of Jim Higginbotham, who wrote the following:

While I have come across some lethal encounters that took a lot of rounds to settle, they mostly were the result of either poor hits (or complete misses) or lack of penetration. Nearly all of the high round count cases I have reviewed involved 9mms, .38s, .357s, or smaller calibers. This is not to say they do not occur with major caliber rounds. It is to say I have been collecting data for 30 years and have not encountered many cases in which multiple hits (more than three, as two or three shots are a fairly normal reflex action) from major caliber cartridges to the center of the chest have not been sufficient . . . and I have not encountered any with the .45, even with ball. I have encountered several with five, six, or even more hits to the center of the chest with .38, .357, 9mm, and .223 rifle rounds failing to stop. Almost every one could be traced to lack of penetration with a couple of exceptions that hit the heart but just did not cause enough damage to be effective quickly. Note I am not talking about "torso" hits. There is a lot of area in the torso in which a hit will seldom produce rapid incapacitation, even if hit by a 12-gauge slug or a 30-06. . . .

A friend of mine killed a Montana elk with his .45 auto, one shot through the heart. It wasn't a man-eating elk, and neither it nor my friend were on mind-altering drugs at the time, but the animal weighed about a thousand pounds, and he wasn't near enough to breathe in my friend's face when he was shot. The scientists and semiscientists and pseudoscientists can have their fun and argue all they want, but I'm sitting in Flagstaff right now, where the earth is covered with four feet of very cold snow, I'm enjoying the firsthand smoke of a good Cuban cigar, and I'll take my 1911s in .45 ACP, thank you very much.

# Condition One and Only

2

**T**exas Ranger Charlie Miller was minding his own business when a concerned citizen came up to him, noted the hammer cocked back on the big 1911 dangling from the ranger's belt, and asked, "Isn't that dangerous?" Charlie replied, "I wouldn't carry the son of a bitch if it wasn't dangerous."

It may be a comment on just how close we are to drowning in the unbearable sensibilities of these overmothering times that the sight of a cocked-and-locked .45 automatic makes some otherwise manly men cover their mouths with a trembling hand. That the hammer is *cocked* is obvious; that the hammer is also *locked* may not be so easy to determine at first glance, especially if you don't know anything about guns, and therein lies the problem of the cocked-and-locked single-action auto as viewed through the worried eyes of those who are uninformed about the important things in life.

Some police departments shy away from the big single-action because they don't trust their officers and they don't want to answer any more questions from gun-ignorant reporters than they have to. Some concealed-carry civilians shy away from the 1911 because they don't trust themselves and they won't bother to get any decent training. Indeed, a cocked-and-locked .45 is as ready looking as a hungry lion lowered on its big paws in preparation for a lunge at Bambi's face, and the sight of it makes some people uneasy, apprehensive, anxious, agitated, downright twitchy.

It should make them happy, confident, relaxed, cheerful, downright serene. After all, the lion is on our side.

Police departments from Florida to California are

embracing the 1911 because they've decided it's the most efficient and effective tool for their difficult jobs. Just recently, the FBI ordered 5,000 45-caliber 1911s from Springfield Armory for its Special Response Team (SRT) units, and LAPD SWAT went with Kimber 1911s. Civilians who care enough about their lives and responsibilities to sign up at a good firearms school for a few days often go directly from the range to a gunshop to buy themselves a 1911 or a good concealment holster to pack the one they've already got. One of the first things these cops and civilians learn is in what condition to carry John Browning's .45 auto.

It is possible to carry a 1911 in three very different conditions. Only one is right. Unless you're one of those guys who wears a baby blue helmet on his head and a decorative pistol with an oversized, unloaded magazine on his hip and is not allowed to think about such things, you have probably already figured this out.

*Condition Three:* chamber empty, hammer down. This requires you to manually cycle the slide before firing. To return the gun to its carry position after firing, you have to drop the magazine, empty the chamber, drop the hammer, and reload and reinsert the magazine, all without shooting an innocent bystander.

Condition Three is a dangerous sop to the excessively squeamish who can't stand the sight of a firearm that looks like it might be usable. As far as I know, the only people who train this way are the Israelis, best known in the handgun world for coming up with the 4 1/2-pound Desert Eagle, an unwieldy and unreliable weapon whose only practical use is firing blanks in low-budget movies about robotic cops.

Such is the irrational fear of a round in the chamber that some idiots who carry their guns in Condition Three advise a technique whereby the slide is retracted, the hammer cocked, and a round chambered by scraping the rear sight along your butt, much in the same manner as striking a kitchen match to light your Kool.

Do not carry your pistol with an empty chamber. Because it is a giant step away from coming to your rescue, it poses a hazard to you and those around you, though not particularly to the criminal who might be attacking you. You

would be better advised to carry a baseball bat, which you are more likely to be able to operate under stress than an unready gun.

*Condition Two:* chamber loaded, hammer down. This requires you to cock the hammer with your thumb before firing, much in the same manner as a single-action revolver whose hammer is very large and uniquely shaped because, quite unlike the hammer of a 1911, its intended purpose is to be cocked by your thumb. Condition Two also requires you to very carefully pull the trigger and lower the hammer over a loaded chamber before returning the gun to its holster.

The technique for manipulating a Condition Two carry is best practiced out in the country in a freshly plowed field, where the bullets will not ricochet off the pavement or the occasional rock every time you decide to reholster your gun. Even more important, carrying a 1911 in Condition Two places an awkward and unnecessary step between you and survival.

*Condition One:* Cocked and locked. Chamber loaded, hammer cocked, thumb safety on. This requires you to snick the safety down before firing and snick it back up when you're finished, a test of manual dexterity that can be mastered in two minutes by any creature equipped with opposable thumbs and probably by a few quadrupeds as well.

The greatest benefit of cocked-and-locked carry, besides instant readiness, is the excellent trigger control it makes immediately available. No other type of semiautomatic can provide the precise and consistent trigger pull of a 1911, trigger pull as fine as can be achieved with the best revolvers operating in single-action mode, straight away available to the shooter with the thumbing down of the safety lever, which is an even more instinctive move than thumbing back a hammer.

Condition One is obviously the fastest way to get your 1911 into action, the least prone to mistakes, the most direct path to precise trigger control, and by far the safest way to carry and operate the gun. It is, therefore, the only way.

That John Browning intended the 1911 to be carried in Condition One is evidenced by the fact that a major feature of the gun is the thumb safety. There is no earthly use for the thumb

This .45 may have a round in the chamber (Condition Two) or it may not (Condition Three). In either case, it is not ready to fire and is in no condition to be carried for defense. A 1911 with the hammer down is even slower to get into action than a single-action revolver, and let's just see you try to fan that little Commander-style hammer. Photo by the author.

safety, the part doesn't even function, unless the hammer is cocked.

It should also be noted that the up/safe, down/fire operation of the single-action 1911 thumb safety is natural, intuitive, and proper. Just to be contrary about it, Carl Walther, who invented the double-action/single-action mechanism with the little Polizei Pistole (PP) in 1929, and S&W, which eventually copied the mechanism and has tried with some success to foist it off on the American public and the law enforcement community ever since, went out of their ways to reverse the safety procedure. On a double-action auto, the thumb lever up means ready to fire (requiring only a very long and godawful trigger pull); thumb lever down drops the hammer on a firing pin block (or right through the block onto the firing pin, as was not uncommon with early S&W 39s). To be fair, it wasn't Carl Walther who designed the double-action PP; it was his son Fritz. Some kids just never learn.

I have always suspected that the ass-backward operation of the thumb safeties of double-actions, at least on the part of their most aggressive promoter, S&W, was a deliberate and premeditated attempt to justify a proprietary marketing claim at the cost of an undetermined number of negligent discharges, which the uninformed call fatal accidents. It certainly makes it extremely difficult to train anybody in the effective use of both single-action and double-action systems (not that it's easy to train anybody in the effective use of the double-action system to begin with).

Since a double-action operates in two different modes, depending on where you find yourself in the shooting cycle, you have to teach two different grips and two different trigger pulls, as well as the transition between them. And you have to decide whether you're going to start and end with the safety on or the safety off, because both methods are taught by different instructors. No ordinary shooter is going to master these beastly routines in two minutes, or maybe ever. There are plenty of extraordinary shooters on the front lines still trying to figure it out.

A widespread cop-out used by popular armchair gun writers who are afraid to carry a cocked-and-locked .45 themselves is to say that the proper operation of a 1911 pistol requires more training than other guns. As usual, the

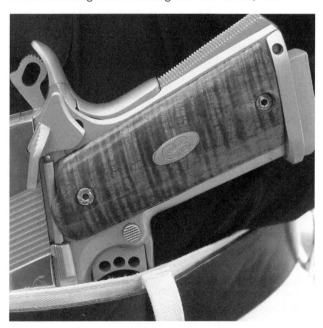

Cocked and locked is how you carry a 1911 if you think you might ever want to use it. Cocked and locked. Get used to it. Photo by Morgan W. Boatman.

popular armchair gun writers have things the other way around. While the operation of anything at all requires some training to ingrain the proper muscle memory, the 1911's single-action mechanism is easier to learn than the double-action/single-action system because it is far less complex and much more instinctive.

Bob Young, vice president of operations at Gunsite, told me that back in the days when he was a U.S. Marine Corps colonel teaching recruits how to shoot 1911s, it took him 4 1/2 days and 500 rounds of ammunition to train a 19-year-old marine to draw his .45 from a tied-down GI flap holster and shoot an adversary twice at seven yards in two seconds flat, including the draw. When he taught double-action Berettas, it took another entire day and an additional 300 rounds, and Young never said whether that 19-year-old

marine could pull off the same two-second routine at the end of it.

For the terminally cocked-and-locked-shy, the well-known 1911 custom shop Cylinder & Slide has come up with a drop-in parts system that changes the way the 1911 thumb safety operates. They call it the Safety Fast Shooting Kit. You carry the 1911 in a condition not possible with an unaltered 1911, sort of a Condition One-and-a-Half: chamber loaded, hammer down, thumb safety on. Uncocked and locked. When you snick the safety off, the hammer suddenly springs up to a cocked position, so you find yourself cocked and unlocked. After firing in the normal manner, you press the hammer down with your other hand —the conversion allows you to push the hammer forward without touching the trigger, so as long as you have your finger off the trigger and the

For the cocked-and-locked-shy, custom gunmaker Kase Reeder makes clear how his pistols are supposed to be carried. Photo by the author.

web of your hand off the grip safety, the normal 1911 passive safeties are engaged as you manually lower the hammer before snicking the thumb safety up and on. Like Condition Two, the converted system requires two hands rather than one thumb to make your pistol safe. I wonder how long it would take to train teenage marines to operate this contraption?

Jeff Cooper dubbed double-action/single-action autos "crunchentickers" because the first double-action shot is a crunch and the follow-up single-action shots are ticks. Faced with this kind of mechanical schizophrenia, something only a deranged mother obsessed with overprotecting her retarded children could come up with, the shooter usually tosses his first shot somewhere out in left field, notwithstanding the fact that, as Max Joseph often says, it's the first shot that counts.

While there is no problem at all in applying 1911 training to pistols devoid of thumb safeties, such as the Glock and the new derivative generation of trigger-cocking, double-action-only autos, there are severe and potentially deadly problems involved when you try to apply that training to pistols with upside-down thumb safeties that operate backward. Is it any wonder that soldiers and cops who know one end of a pistol from the other hurl their Berettas and Smiths at the enemy and trade cold, hard cash and all the fruitcakes and love letters from home for 1911s at every opportunity?

Most standard-issue military officers—that is to say, non-special operations—don't know any more about guns than anybody else. As usual, the shrewd noncoms who actually run every important military operation know exactly how to step over the steaming piles of politically correct bullshit that have been placed in their paths.

I recently received this note from an associate:

A friend served on a tanker ship during the Vietnam War. He comes from a family of shooters. His grandfather competed until late in life at Camp Perry. His two sisters-in-law were on the small-bore rifle team from Tennessee Tech that would have gone to the Moscow Olympics. He and his two brothers have handled both rifles and pistols since they were 8–10 years old.

My friend, call him Bill, was on guard duty as the noncom in charge while in Hong Kong Harbor. The ship was loaded with avgas while on its way to Vietnam. For some reason I don't understand, Navy regs required Bill to carry his .45 with only four rounds in the magazine, nothing in the chamber and uncocked. This set my friend's teeth on edge. He knew better. When he had night duty, he took a fifth round from his pocket, put it in the magazine, and then jacked the "extra" round into the chamber. He then applied the safety . . . Condition One instead of the Navy regulation Condition Three-Minus.

One night, one of the guards on deck yelled, Halt! My friend heard the slap of bare feet on deck as he rounded the corner. He had already drawn the Colt and thumbed off the safety. He too shouted halt as he spotted a shadowy figure headed to the fuel containers.

The figure turned toward Bill while reaching over his shoulder in the classic knife-throwing pose. Bill had already leveled the pistol at him. He fired, sending the figure over the guard chain into Hong Kong Harbor. Bill immediately fired a second shot into the air, released the magazine, and popped out a shell, which went into his pocket. Navy regulations required a warning shot. He had to have two spent cases and two in his weapon.

Bill said that every light on every ship, boat, and sampan in Hong Kong went on between the first and second shots. The Brits were pissed because there was no body since Hong Kong Harbor is a fresh water harbor and the body was well on its way to San Diego by the time they got to his ship.

It's Bill's opinion that had the fuel in the ship been ignited, there would have been a major disaster beyond the tanker he was on. He's also of the opinion had he not carried cocked and locked he would have had a knife sticking in his chest before he could have fired the second shot per regulation.

Here's one final bit of advice to those who believe the cocked-and-locked 1911 is somehow out to get them. In addition to your normal carry pistol, shove a cocked-and-locked—and unloaded—1911 in a holster or your pocket or your underwear or wherever. Check it several times a day to see if it has surreptitiously disengaged its own safety and pulled its own trigger when you weren't looking. After several weeks or months or years of this, draw your own conclusion.

# The Big Fix Nobody Has the Guts to Make

# 3

The pistols John Browning designed before and after the 1911 almost all have one important feature in common, which is the total lack of a peculiar feature found only on a couple of pistols he designed to meet the requirements of the U.S. government in the 1907–1911 time period. John Browning is not responsible for this feature. The government made him do it. It is a feature of, by, and for bureaucrats. It is a feature professional operators of the 1911 negate by whatever means available because, like other unnecessary, ill-advised, overwrought, and imperfect safety devices intended to protect half-wits from their own stupidity, it is dangerous.

The grip safety on a 1911 is just clinging there, waiting to transform your highly effective, lifesaving pistol into nothing more lethal than an oddly shaped 2 1/2-pound rock. It can do this on a whim at any moment. In its own rattling little bureaucratic way, it will laugh at you as you continue to exert pressure on the trigger ever more desperately in a vain attempt to make something positive happen, and it will show no sympathy if you catch a bullet between the eyes while doing so. It undoubtedly delights in its talent to not only annoy people half to death but to actually kill people every chance it gets. Like all exercises in government creativity, it is a total and abject failure. The grip safety of the 1911 is a secret agent of the gunban creatures.

In the days when cavalry soldiers were expected to wield their galloping pistols much as they wielded their sabers, the grip safety may not have been such a big problem. But when Marine Corps Lieutenant Colonel, firearms enthusiast, history professor, race-car driver,

Ride the thumb safety high before, during, and after firing and at all other times when your thumb doesn't have urgent business elsewhere. If this high grip does not fully depress your gun's grip safety 100 percent of the time, tape the grip safety down or pin it or take it to a gunsmith and have it "fixed" like you would a gun-shy dog. Photo by Morgan W. Boatman.

intellectual iconoclast, and all-around stouthearted guy Jeff Cooper came along and started figuring out how best to deploy the sidearm in combat, the grip safety became an issue of potentially life-and-death proportions.

One of the immutable axioms of the Cooper doctrine is that the shooter needs to ride the thumb safety of the 1911 high. The reasons for this require very little reflection to become obvious.

You can only snick the thumb safety down and off when your thumb is resting on top of it. This is, therefore, where your thumb belongs—from the moment you grip your pistol in its holster through your drawstroke and firing sequence until you temporarily move your thumb down to the magazine release button to reload or until you are finished firing and decide to return the safety to the on position, at which point your thumb momentarily glides over and beneath the safety so that you can snick it up. At no other time does your thumb leave its assigned position on top of the thumb safety, and it always returns immediately to its high-riding position and stays there, all set to ready your pistol for firing, until your gun is holstered. This is not a difficult concept to understand, yet many untrained shooters grip their guns with their thumbs planted beneath the thumb safety, where its only possible function is to bounce up into the safety and prevent the weapon from firing. A low-thumb position under heavy recoil often does exactly that.

Now, a high-thumb grip on a 1911, ideally positioned to operate the thumb safety, tends to lessen the pressure the web of your hand exerts on the grip safety. Of course, if the grip safety is not depressed far enough to disengage it, the gun won't fire. This potential calamity is surely the reason the farsighted John Browning did not specify a grip safety for the 1911. The U.S. Army insisted upon the evil-minded little device because some meddling bureaucrat thought it might be a fun idea.

By the way, shooters faced with the operation of the thumb-safety-decocking-lever-entertainment-devices of double-action automatics need not concern themselves with this discussion, because any hope they have of obtaining consistent, controllable, constantly

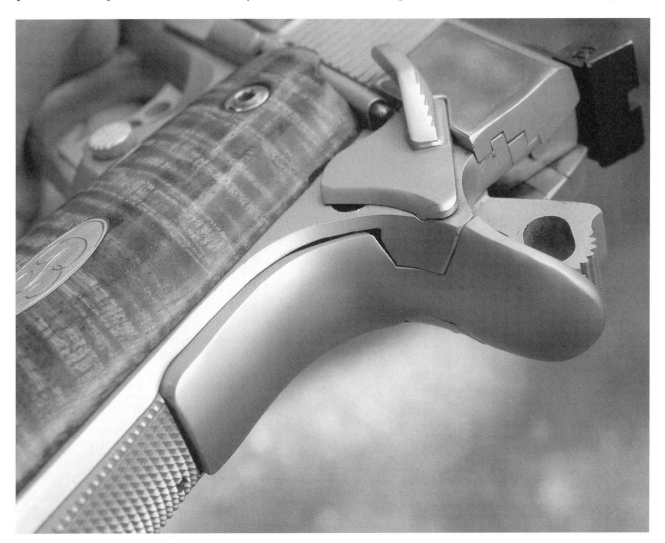

This wasn't John Browning's idea. The grip safety is another typically useless and dangerous government-mandated safety device which should be rendered as dysfunctional as the government bureaucrats who mandated it. Photo by Morgan W. Boatman.

ready, and instantly firing grips on their pistols is nothing but pure fantasy anyway.

The growing number of manufacturers who apparently recognize the problem—notably Kimber, Dan Wesson, Ed Brown, Les Baer, Springfield Armory, the Canadian maker Para-Ordnance, and even the new 1911 builders S&W and SIG (we haven't seen the rumored H&K and CZ 1911s yet)—have decided that the only solution is to implant big, ugly tumors, bulges, bumps, and lumps on their grip safeties so there is no way you can grip the gun in any kind of firing position without pressing the safety all the way down. The Marine Expeditionary Unit (MEU) M1911 used in Iraq also has a widened grip safety with a big lump on it. Before this enhanced gun was issued, the marines had simply taped the grip safety down until the practice was prohibited by the brass, who probably didn't like the color of tape the marines were using. An uncomfortable bulge on the backstrap of your pistol may be a solution of sorts, but it's hardly an elegant one. Tape in any color works more reliably, inelegant or not. The traditional Texas Ranger solution is a strip of rawhide, and I know one trusting soul who uses superglue.

In a recent discussion I had with international firearms instructor Max Joseph, he told me that he disconnects the grip safety of every 1911 he intends to shoot. They're either permanently dropped out or temporarily disabled with medical tape or rubber bands or whatever else is available. "I might miss my grip safety maybe one out of every 500 draws," he says, "and that is one time too many."

Legendary Texas Ranger Manuel Gonzaullas, who *always* carried a brace of 1911s, not only tied down his grip safeties, he never engaged his thumb safeties either, and he sawed off the trigger guards of both guns as well. Gonzaullas was known as Lone Wolf, and nobody, not even when they were backed up by friends and relatives and countrymen, ever messed with him for more than half a second.

You have to wonder about the decision-making executives of gun companies, grown men every one, who are so buffaloed by their own dainty lawyers and the kinds of twits who sue hamburger joints over spilled coffee for a million

bucks. These frightened businessmen are going out of their way to perpetuate an anachronistic little widget that is a safety device in name only, when they could be truly modernizing their guns by returning to the original, unpoliticized purity of the Browning concept. Short of that, virtually every professional 1911 operator of my acquaintance, and there are many, is forced to disable the grip safety by taping it down, pinning it down permanently, adjusting it to the point of practical inoperability, or otherwise making the damnable thing not work.

The grip safety of a 1911, like a three-position thumb safety on a dangerous-game rifle, is a nightmarish gimmick contrived by a committee of people—none of whom has ever fired a gun under stress—who can't imagine why it might be a problem for a shooter absorbed in the process of killing something that's attacking him to just take his mind off what he's doing for a few seconds so he can better admire their clever attempt at making his world safer. While the government monkeys who insisted on the grip safety are long dead, their spawn are apparently alive and well and living in California, where manufacturers of all manner of elegantly designed firearms are now forced to mangle and disfigure their guns with primitive cross-bolt safeties that only a child could manipulate smoothly and that have become the most serious threat to the lives of California shooters. Charging buffalo, murderers, and rapists rejoice—you have the bottomless ignorance of the safety freaks firmly on your side.

If you're the type who breaks into a nervous sweat every time you're tempted to rip the warning tag off your mattress and are therefore apprehensive about disabling the grip safety on your 1911, remember three things: (1) the pistols John Browning designed in 1900, 1902, 1903, and 1905, all of which are clear progenitors of the 1911, did not have grip safeties; (2) the pistol John Browning designed in 1907 (for the army) did have a grip safety, which was called an "auto safety," but it had no thumb safety because to have both would have been patently redundant; (3) the estimable P-35 High Power pistol John Browning designed for Fabrique Nationale (FN) in Belgium for the French military with the aid of FN's chief designer

Dieudonne Saive (a pistol that has achieved even more worldwide acceptance and use than the 1911 and was the last gun John Browning ever designed) functions almost exactly like the 1911 in every way except one. It has no grip safety.

And, just for good measure, the other important Browning-derivative single-action autos of the time—the French MAS-35, the Russian Tokarev, and the Swiss SIG P210—don't have grip safeties either.

The little 1911-pattern Detonics CombatMaster .45 introduced in 1977 dispensed with the grip safety and didn't make a big deal out of it. This was the first small 1911 pistol actually produced in significant numbers, predating the Colt Officer's ACP by almost 10 years. The Detonics drew heavily on Armand Swenson's work with chopped-and-channeled .45s and was, therefore, extremely reliable in operation. It introduced the bushingless, bulged barrel and double and triple recoil springs and was the first 1911 throated and ramped for hollowpoint ammo. The Detonics was an excellent pistol that didn't survive in the marketplace very long, mostly because it was exceedingly expensive, and back in the '70s, only underpaid cops and cheap crooks carried guns. Nevertheless, the Detonics has had a big influence on most concealed-carry guns designed since. It's too bad the unceremonious elimination of the grip safety on the CombatMaster didn't get more attention.

Likewise the 1911-pattern Star PD .45, which

Argentine Ballester-Molina differed from U.S. Government Model 1911 in several ways, the most important of which was a solid frame with no provision for a grip safety. Photo courtesy of Hakan's Custom Grips.

was my carry gun throughout the '80s, until my house burned down and the PD's aluminum frame literally melted. I loved that little Spanish Star, because it was light, compact, and, most especially, had no grip safety.

My first .45 was an Argentine Ballester-Molina, a wonderful rendition of the 1911 that was all the better for its lack of a grip safety. It wasn't mutilated with a firing-pin block "safety" either. I sure wish I had kept that one.

The shakiest of concepts, when they get ingrained through simple repetition into the way we look at things, are hard to eradicate. I have not yet been able to persuade any gun maker I know today to eradicate the grip safety of the 1911, as shaky a concept as there ever was. Gun makers tell me they're afraid some shithead lawyer will say to the jury, "This reckless person removed a safety device from his gun and that's why that poor criminal was accidentally shot." The riposte is, of course, "No, I'm a very careful person, and I removed a gratuitous doohickey from my gun that could easily have prevented its safe and effective deployment, and that's why that poor criminal was not able to disembowel his victim before I deliberately shot him twice in the chest with my .45."

If there's a gun maker out there with the guts to make a new 1911 frame with a backstrap as slick as a High Power, I'd like to hear from him. Otherwise, I'm in the market for a mint-condition Ballester-Molina the Argentines used to make. Anybody who knows how to tango knows better than to screw up a perfectly good gun.

John Browning did not spoil the form or function of his P-35 High-Power with an ill-advised grip safety only a gunban creature could love. Photo courtesy of The Robar Companies.

# The Doctrine 4

The U.S. Army at the beginning of the 20th century, the environment within which John Browning designed the 1911 pistol, was a far cry from the military forces now at the beginning of the 21st century. Recruits of that era surely had more general gun knowledge than the TV-educated generations of today, but what handgun experience they had was almost exclusively with single-action revolvers. The semiautomatic pistol was a radically new and different instrument indeed.

In those days a soldier was expected to carry his pistol fully secured in an enclosed flap holster and, in the event that he should ever want to use the gun, it was assumed he would grab it with his right hand and hold it out at arm's length in order to get the muzzle as far away from his horse and as close to his target as possible. Flap holsters have not gone away, but all the horses have. And, thanks primarily to the efforts of one man, today's military recognizes that a soldier is a bipedal creature equipped with two arms, two hands, and opposable thumbs.

The man, of course, is U.S. Marine Lt. Col. Jeff Cooper. He explains,

> In the beginning the pistol was a cavalry weapon—an attempt to extend the reach of both saber and lance. Thus it was a tool to be used with one hand, the other being needed to control the horse. Quickly, however, it was discovered to be the equalizer, as effective afoot as ahorse. Despite this, its ancestry ruled for a couple of centuries, and armies continued to regard it as one-handed clear up into the late 20th century.

Then came practical shooting, the revolution, and the one-hand gun evolved into the two-hand gun. The revolution was born in southern California, at Big Bear Lake, and I know about it because I was intimately involved in it.

Cooper was more than involved in the revolution; he was the driving force behind it, the official leader of it, and, to this day, its chief spokesman, philosopher, and spiritual conscience. What the revolution produced, in the early 1960s, is called The Modern Technique of the Pistol. John Browning has surely been smiling in his grave ever since, undoubtedly relieved that somebody finally figured out how to use the instrument he invented far ahead of its time.

The Modern Technique is an intensive training doctrine that is taught today by Cooper's former pupils at Gunsite Ranch in Arizona, Max Joseph and TFTT in California, Louis Awerbuck of Yavapai Firearms Academy in Arizona, Clint Smith at the new Thunder Ranch operation in Oregon, a few other proper firearms training academies around the world, the U.S. Marine Corps, virtually all military special forces, and elite law enforcement teams here and abroad.

To one degree or another, the things being taught today about pistol handling and shooting to cops, soldiers, other armed professionals and civilians worldwide are things discovered on the front lines of Jeff Cooper's revolution. After a week of such training under a capable and hopefully gifted instructor such as the ones named above, you would be the odds-on favorite in any shootout with a highly trained soldier from 1911, 1921, 1931, 1941, 1951, 1961, or, for the most part, even after that. The difference in effectiveness is that great because the shift in technique, while appearing to be the simplest and most natural thing in the world, was truly that radical. Cooper says,

When recovering from a shattered radius at the Marine Corps base in Quantico in 1947, I "audited" the FBI Academy and ran right into what the Bureau called its "Practical Pistol Course,"

which, while hardly practical, was a great step forward from conventional target shooting. In company with Howie Taft (then captain, later colonel), I dreamed up a military course of fire for the pistol, which was especially suited for infantrymen of all grades whose duties precluded the packing of a rifle—drivers, mechanics, tankers, artillerymen, staff officers, etc. Target shooting did not do this. We sought improvement.

But the war ended, and as a civilian (sort of) I wound up at Big Bear Lake in California, where I continued to play around with the practical pistol. Contests were organized, beginning with a straightforward quick-draw match called "The Leatherslap," which everyone enjoyed and became an annual event. Contestants wanted more, so a monthly program began which emphasized variety and realism. No two matches [of the same design] could be held in the same year, and the challenges should replicate actual gunfights—so far as practical.

Of the many highly evolved tenets of The Modern Technique, four are immutable. They have been so thoroughly proven in real life that only a fool would disregard them, which is not to say that they are never disregarded. Two of these are covered in Chapter 2: Condition One and Only, about cocked-and-locked carry, and Chapter 3: The Big Fix Nobody Has the Guts to Make, which addresses the importance of riding the thumb safety high. The remaining two, which are discussed here, have to do with the Weaver stance and the business of sighting. Each of these keystones of The Modern Technique rests on a broad mental foundation that is covered in Chapter 5: Mind-set.

## THE WEAVER STANCE IS THE FIGHTING STANCE

Cooper says this of his original Big Bear group:

The creative genius was Jack Weaver, a deputy sheriff and pistol hobbyist, who observed, thought it over, and concluded that two hands are better than one. He placed seventh the first year, then came back the second year and wiped us out. Some were using the cowboy hip-shot, some the Applegate "instinctive" method, and I was shooting one-handed long-point from the target range. Jack walloped us all, and decisively, using a six-inch Smith K-38. He was very quick, and he did not miss. And, of course, he shot from the Weaver stance, which was, and is, the way to go.

The Weaver stance—which includes the two-handed grip, the application of isometric tension by the arms, and aggressive positioning of the body, legs, and feet—is very much like most other classic martial arts stances, save for the grip of the gun itself. You'll see the same principles applied in other forms of combat, from boxing to karate to spear-throwing, because of the obvious benefits offered, including flexibility, control, compactness, body dynamics, directed strength, and did I mention flexibility?

Still, even today, some instructors continue to teach the isosceles, a Gumby-like stance, which works best if the objective is to plant the shooter

The fighting Weaver stance demonstrated by the author. This is the stance that warriors have used for at least 5,000 years. Photos by Morgan W. Boatman.

This is the isosceles or Gumby stance demonstrated by the author's dumb twin brother. Note the resemblance of the shooter's body to a popular handgun target. The Pepper popper, so named by Jeff Cooper in honor of its inventor, John Pepper, is a steel reactive target widely used in competition games worldwide. Louis Awerbuck criticizes the Pepper popper because it is much too easy to hit, whereas others recommend that the shooter emulate it whenever possible. Photos by Morgan W. Boatman.

in one place and make him the biggest, slowest-moving target possible, sort of like a life-size Pepper popper.

Such a questionable stance is necessary only if your breasts are so large they interfere with normal body movement, an affliction that is apparently widespread among modern FBI recruits of both sexes and must be the reason they currently train this way.

To be fair, the isosceles stance comes naturally to the casual plinker or limp-wristed, stiff-armed target shooter firing downloaded practice rounds, and it is perhaps easier for the inexperienced to acquire under range conditions. It will do for shooting scenarios that are based on small-caliber handguns and do not include any remote possibility that you might need to advance; retreat; shoot from side to side, over, or under; make a fast 90- or 180-degree swing; seek concealment; or take cover at any time during the imagined or real firefight. Otherwise, the graceless inflexibility of the isosceles makes it as life threatening to the shooter as the Weaver is to the target.

The Weaver not only gives you the strongest isometrically reinforced recoil-controlling grip possible, a crucial factor if you're shooting full-power .45 ACP loads, it also allows you to quickly pivot on one foot to cover any adversary's position—fixed, moving, multiple, up, down, through a small opening, around the corner, or appearing out of thin air, which is something adversaries have been known to do.

## THINK ONLY ABOUT THE FRONT SIGHT

Cooper and company, in their quest for fast and accurate fire, quickly discovered that "instinctive" shooting was anything but. Simply pointing a gun at something, as in the infamous "FBI crouch" of bygone days, was not a very good way to make sure the thing you wanted to shoot got shot. Granted, some individual shooters with years of intensive practice could pull it off. The quick-draw artists you used to see at the circus could achieve their trick shots too, as long as their guns were loaded with blanks. Unsighted fire was something that came naturally to almost nobody, and, factoring in the requirements for power and accuracy as well as speed, it did not work at any distance beyond powder-burn range. There's a reason rifles and pistols are equipped with sights, which is not just so you can pop the eyeball out of a squirrel 300 yards distant, and it can be a fatal mistake not to use them and use them properly. You can be assured that a professional hunter facing the murderous charge of a Cape buffalo uses the sights on his 470 Nitro Express. And his target is considerably larger than any you're likely to encounter in a back alley or your bedroom.

One of my favorite Jeff Cooper quotes is, "Blessed are those who, in the face of death, think only about the front sight." Shooting well, especially in a life-threatening situation, requires an enormous amount of concentration. Only a depth of training will direct you to automatically concentrate on the right thing, the thing that will save your life, that thing known as the front sight.

With iron sights and cellular eyeballs, you can choose only one of these three sight pictures. Use Option A (left) if you need to concentrate on removing a piece of lint from your rear sight. Use Option B (center) if you're waiting to be formally introduced to your adversary before beginning the fight. Otherwise, use Option C (right) and get on with it. Photos by the author and Morgan W. Boatman.

Iron sights present three possible planes for your viewing pleasure—the rear sight, the front sight, and the target. Eyes being what they are, in your need to align these three planes you can only focus on one of them. Focus on the rear sight makes the front sight fuzzy and the target little more than a ghost image. Focus on the target renders both sights useless. Focus on the front sight gives you a fuzzy but usable rear sight and still allows you to identify vital areas on your target. There is only one possible choice. When your target is shooting at you, however, there is a very strong instinctive urge to focus on that, thus the need for concentration cultivated by training.

There are instructors who don't believe the human mind is capable of such discipline and who therefore advocate hip shooting, point shooting, the Hollywood concept of "instinctive" shooting. In other words, just thrust your gun out there and pull the trigger. This technique can be relied upon only if, when you thrust your gun out there, your adversary grabs it in his hands, drags it into his mouth, and starts sucking on the muzzle while you pull the trigger. Otherwise, you're in trouble, because you won't be shooting to make a hit, you'll be shooting to contravene your panic.

There is plenty of African hunting literature that includes instances where otherwise fine shots with years of experience shooting squirrels at 300 yards have been known to miss entire elephants at 10 feet. If you are out of powder-burn range, which is about the same as spitting distance, the only thing you can rely on to save your life is your front sight.

## THE FACTS OF 1911 LIFE

Carry your weapon cocked and locked and ready for anything. Ride the thumb safety high for instant response and complete control. Take a flexible fighting stance. Focus on the sight plane that will deliver the most vital hits.

This is not simple dogma. These are proven

You will never see this in real life. Only trick photography can bring rear sight, front sight, and target into focus at the same time. Photos by the author and Morgan W. Boatman.

principles developed and perfected for the 1911 pistol that, like most other things developed on that timeless platform, also apply, in principle, to every other firearm intended as a practical tool.

There are some who say these principles apply to life in general. Think about it.

# Mind-set 5

**A**pparently, it is extremely difficult if not well nigh impossible under any circumstances whatsoever for a conventionally balanced human being loaded down with contemporary social values to destroy the life of a fellow human being by deliberately shredding his vital organs with a .45 slug. Not considering myself a member of that timorous group, I must say that their lack of basic instinct and animal courage has always puzzled me. It is nevertheless true. I have talked at length with firearms instructors from every armed discipline at every level of instruction, and they unanimously confirm the problem.

In World War II, only 15 to 20 percent of American riflemen were able to deliberately kill an enemy soldier with aimed fire. In Vietnam, American soldiers fired 55,000 rounds for every enemy soldier they killed. Military analysts estimate that 80 to 85 percent of soldiers cannot kill another human being if they are directly accountable for it. Twenty percent of law enforcement applicants openly admit they could not or would not shoot a violent assailant even to save another officer's life.

Jeff Cooper summed up the relationship between mind-set and marksmanship pretty well when he said, "One of the best examples of technique I can recall is, a couple came home one night over in West Los Angeles, and they were greeted on the second deck by a creep with a gun. The creep says to the man, 'Lie down on the floor.' He was going to tie him up with tape, and so the guy lets him do it. While the creep is tying the guy's hands the girl reaches around and pulls the pistol out of the creep's waistband and kills

A favorite Cooper quote: "If violent crime is to be curbed, it is only the intended victim who can do it. The felon does not fear the police, and he fears neither judge nor jury. Therefore, what he must be taught to fear is his victim." Photo by Morgan W. Boatman.

United States. Any class you take at Gunsite includes use of the simulators. We use very realistic targets and have the simulators set for the level of class you're in. In those simulators, you have people that you're not supposed to shoot. And if you do, the instructor's going to stop you and you're going to have a talk about that. You just did something very wrong, and the police are coming, and the district attorney is coming—it's better to learn it here, because if you don't you could get in trouble."

When Young says that the shoot and no-shoot targets used in Gunsite's simulators are realistic,

him with it. Now, I don't know how good a shot she was, but she was good enough."

I've quoted this Cooper statement before, and I'll quote it again: "Mind-set is everything. A willingness to take the step."

Cooper went on to say, "Obviously, if you're a good shot your self-confidence takes care of itself. You know you can do it. You don't have to worry about it. If you want a bullet in that teacup over there and you know you can do it every time in a second and a half, the decision to do it is much easier. It's comparable to flying a piston-engine fighter plane. It's not, how am I going to fly this airplane? You just wish the airplane and it goes, it goes where you want it. That's difficult to teach."

Nevertheless, hands-free flying is what a firearms instructor must be able to teach his serious students. All technique must grow out of mind-set. "Far more important [than brilliant pistolcraft] is attitude, the state of mind necessary to do what is needful when the time arises," Cooper said. "The best shot in the world is helpless if he doesn't want to shoot."

Any person who deserves to survive in this world is born with a strong killer instinct and spends the rest of his life refining it. Focused combat firearms training hones it to a fine edge.

Bob Young, the retired U.S. Marine Corps colonel who is head of operations at Gunsite, says, "Jeff Cooper pioneered the use of simulators and built some of the first shooting houses in the

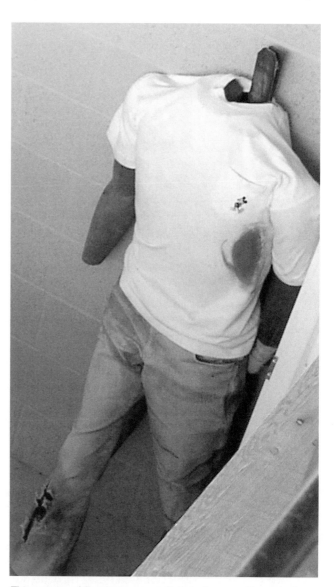

This was one of Gunsite's more realistic bad guys until somebody blew his mind-set out the window. Photo by the author.

he means realistic. They have heads and upper bodies, wear shirts, hats, wigs, and guns. They practically grin at you over your sights. Pulling the trigger on one of these characters is an entirely different experience from pulling the trigger on a cardboard cutout. It's the same at TFTT and Yavapai Firearms Academy and Thunder Ranch. It's not shooting people, but it's as close as we can come without playing holy hell with the budget.

Young says, "These things really do generate stress. People come out of there with wet armpits and elevated pulse rates." Unlike in real life, however, they do always come out.

Making a series of rapid life-and-death decisions, simulated or real, puts the human mind into overdrive. It is perhaps the most important shooting exercise you can undertake. If you are not capable of learning from it, if you are one of the overwhelming majority of people who is not capable of killing when the situation demands it (an undeniable fact that I still find extremely difficult to believe despite the evidence), then you should just go home and stay out of the way of those who are more capable than you.

On the other hand, if you have what it takes in terms of mind-set, attitude, killer instinct if you will, then training in technique will allow you to put a bullet in a teacup in a second and a half any time there is an urgent need to rearrange the china.

# How Important $6$ Is Training?

## And What Does Competition Have to Do with It?

**I** once knew a guy who went down to the local sporting goods store and bought a brand new Gold Cup. He took it out to the range, put a loaded magazine in it, and fired seven large holes in a nearby piece of paper. He then put the Colt back in the box, took it home, placed it unloaded in a battery-operated handgun safe in his bedroom, hid the box of 13 remaining cartridges under his socks in a dresser drawer, and declared himself prepared to defend his family. Now, I don't consider this guy an amateur or a subamateur or a hobbyist or a beginner or even a greenhorn or anything like that, because he resides about four stories beneath the lowest of those levels, so there's no need to say any more about him, except to point out that there are too many guys like him and that none of them are reading this book.

For those who are a lot higher up on the evolutionary scale, certainly high enough to fill the slot of serious amateur, a few words about training with your 1911 is in order.

There are those who believe that because a 1911 has a simple on-off thumb safety and a relatively light single-action trigger pull, it requires more training than most other handguns for a level of competency to be achieved. There are others, myself included, who believe that because a 1911 does not have a multi-function safety lever/decocker and a multi-function trigger with both double-action and single-action pulls, it requires less training than most other handguns for a level of competency to be achieved. In all cases, a certain amount of intensive training in the basic manipulation of your gun's mechanical controls is obviously required. But, if competency in pistolcraft is your goal, such fundamentals are only the beginning.

Jeff Cooper said, "When I began to teach pistolcraft, first at Big Bear, then at Gunsite, I emphasized variety, realism, and the Weaver stance. I thought that I covered the subject, but I ran into a theoretical obstacle. I discovered that there is a basic divergence in purpose between the amateur and the professional. The amateur seeks excellence. The professional seeks adequacy. The hobbyist shooter wants to be better. The cop wants to be good enough."

Feeling lucky, punk?
Photo by Tony Mandile.

To put a somewhat different spin on it, all too often the amateur wants to become a better marksman so he can do trick shots and impress his friends; the intelligent professional wants to be able to survive a gunfight. And therein lies a wide spot in the road that can fork off in two different directions or continue on toward the horizon with a broader perspective of the surrounding countryside.

Ask a seasoned African hunter what the most important elements are in bringing down dangerous game, and he will reply that accurate shot placement is first, appropriate bullet design and construction second, and caliber third. Though he is fully aware of it, he will often forget to mention the hunt itself, the planning and the stalk that give the hunter crucial advantages of position, range, surprise, trajectory angle, and rifle stability that precede shot placement.

The amateur pistol shooter often forgets to mention such tactical preparation as well—not because he assumes you already know that but because he himself does not know such a thing exists—and will rush on to a discussion of the importance of accuracy, skip over the significance of bullet design because he only needs to punch a hole in a piece of cardboard, and launch into a lecture on caliber liberally sprinkled with quotes from ads and advertorials out of a recent newsstand gun magazine.

The professional, on the other hand, may sell the importance of his individual performance

short because, in the back of his mind, he's counting on backup by a full team armed with sniper rifles, submachine guns, and night-vision optics.

Good training can straighten out all such mind warps. Mediocre training can cast every deadly wrinkle in bronze.

Quite frequently the hero loses his status as the master practitioner of tactics and becomes the target instead. With a hair-raising roar and yellow fangs gleaming, a 500-pound lion hurtles toward your head with the momentum of a cannonball. Out of the next dark doorway a man suddenly appears with a six-inch blade glowing in the moonlight and moving inexorably in your direction. You will not choose these times to sit on a rock and meditate, to initiate a rational dialogue with yourself or your attacker, or to review the notes you took in Tactics 101. The world is suddenly a very simple place, and there are no decisions to be made. Your intellectual ability to deliberately manipulate your environment has been replaced by a more immediate and dominant force. Whether your training is good, mediocre, highly advanced, or practically nonexistent, you will now operate under its complete and automatic guidance.

The lack of training often leads to situations that are comic or tragic, depending on your viewpoint. There was the champion target shooter who went to Africa to hunt dangerous game for the first time. From no more than 35 yards, he made a perfect broadside shot on a large Cape buffalo bull that, shot perfectly or not, immediately turned and charged. The response of the target shooter-hunter was to drop to the ground and curl up in a fetal position with his thumb in his mouth. There was the cop, suddenly faced with an enraged aggressor, who drew his service pistol and, in record-setting rapid fire, emptied his 17-round magazine into the floor to prevent his intimidating foe from taking it away and shooting him with it.

Choose your training course and your instructor well while you have the time to indulge in such luxuries, because you will be programming your future response to a life-threatening situation. Which means, among other things, if you intend to carry a gun for defense do not go to a school run by a competition shooter no matter how many championship match titles he may have won. Defending yourself and others with gunfire is not a game. Specialized skills developed within the confines of artificial rules and regulations seldom converge with the unpredictable demands of reality.

You don't go to racing school to learn to drive in the real world; you go to racing school to learn to race. After a day of keeping your foot in it on a closed circuit where other highly focused drivers at about the same level of skill are going at very nearly the same speed, all in the same direction, on an otherwise empty track, it's a shock when you get in your passenger car at the end of the day and enter big-city rush-hour traffic. Drivers at all of the lower levels of competence come at you at varying speeds from all different directions, talking on the phone, kissing their girlfriends, eating chicken, and drinking coffee. Makes you want to escape to the safety of the high-speed race course as fast as you can.

Racing school doesn't teach you a thing about any of this. You can't just get out in front and go fast because there's a wall of cars in front of you. You can't use the whole road because there's the inconvenience of oncoming traffic. You can't cut the apex of the upcoming curve because there's a pickup full of watermelons sitting there. You can't stand on the brakes just before you turn the wheel because the guy driving the Cadillac on your tail is watching a puppy eat the pants off a little girl on a billboard. You can't accelerate out of the turn unless you want to drive up the ramp of the transport truck rumbling along in front of you. The fact that you can go like the wind on the high banked curve of a fenced-off road course will not prevent your cruise down the boulevard from being interrupted by a teenage girl lurching out of a parking lot and planting her father's Lincoln Town Car in your passenger seat.

Things you learn to do under controlled conditions rarely have much bearing on day-to-

day reality. Still, we all want to know just how fast we can really go, don't we?

Many shooters, having gone through a thorough firearms training course, go on to compete in one of the combat handgun venues, IPSC or IDPA, as a way of keeping their marksmanship active and gun handling honed. Unfortunately, the game-winning techniques and skills they soon learn that are relevant only in a competitive environment become part of their training, whether they intend them to or not. It takes a strong will to remain tactically correct when others are cutting every tactical corner to game their scores. There's nothing wrong with playing dirty; in fact, it is to be encouraged in real-world scenarios, but you have to make sure you don't get your priorities confused and end up

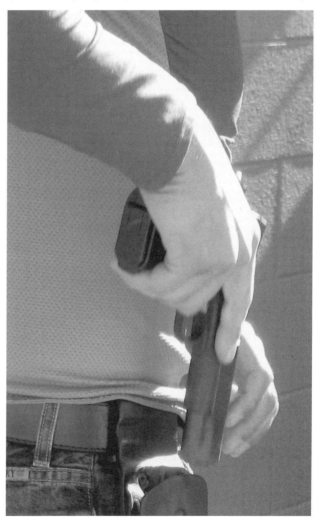

Is this training? Is this a game? Is this for real? Photo by the author.

"If you wish to become a really good shot you will learn to live with your gun." Photo by Morgan W. Boatman.

just cheating yourself. There's winning, and then there's winning.

Have you heard the story about the hot-shot competition shooter who, faced with the real armed and shaggy thing, drew his gun, jumped out from behind hard cover to face his attacker, and started to execute a tactical reload without having got so far as pulling the trigger? He died with two full magazines in his hand, a cold 230-grain hollowpoint in the chamber of his gun, and a tiny 22-caliber hole between his eyes.

Training and competition, like higher education, can cultivate your natural abilities and anchor them on a foundation of knowledge and wisdom. They can also inflict you with that college-kid mentality that leads you to believe that, because you beat Harry in a Mozambique drill last Saturday, that pair of druggies scooting toward you out of the alley can do you no harm. Unless your ambition is to spend your life playing

stylized games, do not make the move from defensive reality to the shooting equivalent of narrow academia. Haven't you noticed that the longer a person stays on a college campus the dumber he or she gets?

You'll do better in some environments than others. If you want to be a lawyer, God forbid, you can probably get all the credits you need at the University of Wisconsin, but you'd be better advised to try to get into Yale. You can learn something about shooting from anybody who knows more than you do, but you'll learn the really important things from people who have seen the elephant and brought back its tail, people like Louis Awerbuck, Max Joseph, and Clint Smith.

Some people feel that a permit to carry a concealed weapon (CCW) is proof of their abilities with a handgun, when it is actually only proof that they have caved in to the government one more time and forked over a political fee for the temporary privilege of exercising their most fundamental natural right. If you carry a gun, with or without a CCW, it is nobody's responsibility but yours to make sure you are competent in its intended use.

Go to driving school, not racing school. You're not going to enter the next Formula One race in Monte Carlo, but you need to be able to navigate to the grocery store and back without wandering off the road into a ditch. Get a good foundation in combat firearms training, indulge yourself in high-pressure competition until you figure out where true wisdom dwells, drop out of the system, and pursue it on your own.

Advanced education is that which you discover yourself.

Jeff Cooper says, "If you wish to become a really good shot you will learn to live with your gun. It should always be within reach, and you should handle it freely. Not every household is the same, but if you maintain your rifle within reach at your breakfast table you will get in the amount of dry practice necessary to become totally one with your weapon. With the pistol you should try five dry snaps before you put it on in the morning and five more before you take it off in the evening. This way you will eventually blend with the piece, and your skill will be something unconscious and undirected. Note that you cannot shoot 'instinctively.' The shooting stroke is a programmed reflex, and you program it only by familiarity. You cannot go to the range enough to program those reflexes, but you can instill them at home, and the master marksman does just that."

Live with your gun.

# Gunning through Gunsite

**7**

**Y**ou can tell the difference between students who come here to train their minds and bodies in life-saving disciplines and those to whom there is little difference between Gunsite and Disneyland. The latter approach every shooting and gun-handling exercise as though they were vying with their classmates to win some giant stuffed mouse to improve their living room decor, the former with the concentrated intent of getting good enough before the end of the week to blow the stuffing right out of the big rat and all the other rodent-like creatures in his pack. Mindset.

The only tourists this week were gone after three days. The ones who stayed were more substantial. There was the lady from the East Coast who was being stalked and threatened by a vicious former boyfriend. A bright young cop from California was assuming responsibility for his own firearms training, since his department provided little of quality. An undercover federal agent was here as R&R for an undisclosed job well done. Several shooters were taking the course for the second or third time, gradually improving their already considerable skills. There was a martial arts master over from the United Kingdom just to get a fresh breath of lead- and-powder-scented air because his own country prohibits him from even owning a handgun, as it prohibits him from defending himself and his family with his well-trained hands. There were pairs of best friends, mates, brothers, fathers and sons, all come to taste one of the original crucibles of humankind.

Course 250 at Gunsite Academy, Basic Defensive Pistol, is an intensive, weeklong training regimen dedicated to the

Guns used in this class were almost all 1911s and Glocks, with the odd SIG and Beretta. Photo by the author.

tactical deployment of powerful handguns that prepares students to handle, manipulate, control, and shoot more effectively than any standard law enforcement or military course of training. Courses of equally high value that I personally know of are offered by TFTT in California and Thunder Ranch in Oregon.

This looked like a particularly good class. There were 20 students, 20 guns, half 1911s, the other half Glocks, with the exception of an agency-required Beretta and a couple of SIGs. The team of six instructors was led by Louis Awerbuck, a world-class shooter, thinker, writer, and instructor who served in 1 Special Services

Adjunct Instructor Il Ling New demonstrates a quick kneeling position. Photo by the author.

Battalion in the South African Defence Force. Each of the adjunct instructors was fully capable of leading the class on his (or her) own: Michel Rothlisberger, who looked fresh out of high school but is a colonel in the Swiss army and head of Switzerland's vaunted handgun training program; Il Ling New, a delicate beauty of no more than a hundred pounds who grew up helping her father guide big-game hunters in remote wilderness areas all over the country and who could undoubtedly take a grizzly bear apart in three seconds flat; Steve McDaniel, down from Alaska;

The little time that is spent in the classroom is important nevertheless. Here Range Master and Chief Instructor Louis Awerbuck explains some fine points. Photo by the author.

Doug Day; Alice Rogers. Quite a team.

The first order of business on the first day was a brief classroom session where the rules were laid down. Awerbuck held up a toy pistol that reminded me of my Dick Tracy model from days gone by. He explained that he would sometimes appear to break the ironclad gun-handling safety rules with this gun-shaped object in order to make a point, and he wanted everyone in the room to be satisfied that it was indeed a toy, not a gun at all. He asked if anyone wanted to inspect the plaything to be sure. No one responded, and that was lesson number one.

"Never ever again take anybody's word that the thing he's holding in his hand that looks like a gun is harmless," Awerbuck told the class. The

Fast and accurate fire with major-caliber handguns is what Gunsite is all about. Photo by the author.

Louis Awerbuck is acknowledged as one of the best firearms instructors in the world. Photo by the author.

black plastic thing was then passed around to all the students, everyone dropping the little magazine designed to hold soft plastic BBs, racking the plastic slide back and forth to clear any BBs that might be lurking inside, sticking their fingers down into the action to make sure, watching their muzzle control, treating the thing as though it might be loaded with invisible 45-caliber Black Talons. Good lesson.

The shooting started right away. At distances from 3 to 25 yards, students drilled in the drawstroke, fast and accurate fire, reloading,

clearing malfunctions, shooting from different positions. Under the quiet direction of Louis Awerbuck and with personal attention from the other five instructors, each shooter started gradually pulling together the three elements of Jeff Cooper's Combat Triad: mind-set, the ability to control a dangerous environment; marksmanship, accurate fire delivered under pressure; and gun handling—as Awerbuck stressed, it is not bad shooting that gets people killed so much as it is the lack of good gunhandling skills. Awerbuck never let an opportunity pass without reminding students that losers in gunfights most often come in second (that is, dead last) because "most people beat themselves."

"Your weapon is your mind," he said more than once. "Your gun is your tool. A lethal confrontation with firearms is about strategy and tactics, not just shooting." Awerbuck knows that of which he speaks.

As the hours and days wore on, shooters moved from the square range to the outdoor

Students quickly learn that smooth is fast. Photo by the author.

simulators or "jungle walks" to the nerve-racking indoor simulators and house-clearing exercises. Targets changed from the plain, tan IPSC style that encourages focus on the front sight, to camouflage patterns that challenge recognition of center body mass, to realistic depictions of criminals, hostages, innocent bystanders, and little old ladies with sawed-off shotguns to force target identification and accurate shot placement, to reactive steel Pepper poppers of both good-guy and bad-guy varieties. Shooters fired their weapons under stress in the light and heat of the high desert sun, in the treacherous glow of twilight, and in the dark of night. There were man-on-man "duels" that tested speed of the draw, accuracy and follow-through, the smoothness of reloads, and the sheer nerve of the contestants.

Col. Bob Young had told me that, before he became vice president of operations at Gunsite, he trained his security force marines here and that after four and a half days and 500 rounds of ammunition a marine could draw his 45-caliber 1911 from his tied-down GI flap holster and shoot an adversary twice at seven yards in two seconds. After five days and almost 1,500 rounds of ammo, most of these students could do the same, and their confidence showed. They could not be outshot, even by most marines. But, as Awerbuck pointed out, the danger was that if they didn't use their heads they might very well be out-thought.

"The teacher must first of all know *why*," Jeff Cooper had said. Louis Awerbuck never directed a student to do anything without explaining the real-life reasons behind it. The lesson-filled

Col. Bob Young, Gunsite vice president, and the author overlook a 360-degree indoor simulator, also known as a "kill house." Photo by Morgan W. Boatman.

If Awerbuck asks you to try something a little different, he'll tell you exactly why. Photo by the author.

anecdotes he had to tell were alone worth the price of admission to Course 250.

Stereotyping, or "profiling," is a natural human trait and can be very useful. If you follow your initial instincts you will likely be right. And sometimes you will be wrong. A local sheriff responded to a major shootout between a gang of scruffy bikers and a bunch of guys in suits. Immediately joining in the gun battle on the side of the guys in suits, the sheriff personally killed two undercover federal agents and helped a gang of well-dressed armed robbers escape. As far as this sheriff was concerned, however, there wasn't much difference between federal agents and armed robbers.

Dry-firing has always been a staple routine to aid rapid sight acquisition and trigger control. The head of a major law enforcement agency was practicing dry-firing at a target on the wall in his office. He had no sooner finished practice and reloaded his .357 Magnum revolver with high-velocity hollowpoints than the phone rang. After a long and heated telephone conversation he went back to what he was doing, dry-firing into his

office wall. When his second-in-command, sitting at his desk in the office next door, caught a bullet in the brain, the shooter's brilliant career in law enforcement came to a sudden halt as well, and he went on to become one of the most famous gun writers of all time.

There are signs in all of the restroom facilities at Gunsite explaining the "why" of certain necessary procedures. For instance, you are expected to close the door when you leave because, if you don't, some wild desert critter is likely to seek shelter in the protected space, find itself trapped, and unintentionally set up a terrifying ambush for the next person entering. The restrooms are not meant to be simulators and are not equipped to withstand gunfire.

The thought processes underlying what some first-time students had previously considered the simple act of pulling the trigger tell you that it would be a good idea to prepare yourself by reading not only Jeff Cooper (and Awerbuck's own book, *Tactical Reality,* Paladin Press, 1999) but by studying the works of Sun Tzu and Carl von Clausewitz as well. Sun Tzu reveals such

Successful graduation from Gunsite still earns a visit with Colonel Cooper. Photo by the author.

kernels of Chinese wisdom as, "All warfare is based on deception." The great Prussian soldier and writer von Clausewitz presents you with ideas such as, "In war everything is uncertain and variable, intertwined with psychological forces and effects, and the product of a continuous interaction of opposites."

These philosophical axioms of combat see practical application at Gunsite. They are important things for you to know before you strap on a .45 and sally forth into the real world.

Many students, especially law enforcement types, are surprised to look at house-clearing exercises the other way around. No one, not even a cop, will likely ever face the prospect of entering

a house alone where one or more armed adversaries are known to lie in wait. It is quite possible, however, that you could someday find yourself inside a house suddenly containing such threats and have to fight your way out. The necessity for "cutting the pie" and other techniques practiced in the 360-degree simulators now comes into stark focus.

Some are surprised, as well, when they realize the fastest reload or malfunction clearance is often a second gun. Malfunctions in this class were few, however, and jams nonexistent, even among the tightly fitted "match" guns that are frequently plagued by reliability problems. Awerbuck himself is known to routinely carry a

45-caliber 1911 as primary and a 9mm Glock as backup, covering his bets in both directions.

A truism among African dangerous-game hunters is, "It's the dead ones that kill you." This wisdom comes from not uncommon experiences such as shooting an elephant in the head with a big-bore rifle, missing the brain by a fraction of an inch, but delivering a Mike Tyson KO punch that lays the giant pachyderm out flat, dead to the world . . . until you climb up on top of it so your PH can take your hero picture; or blowing the lungs and heart out of a Cape buffalo, sure of your shot, watching it fall, feeling victorious until the buffalo decides he wants to get even more than he wants to die and, drawing on that mysterious reserve life-force that seems capable of sustaining African buffalo even when all mechanical life-support systems are destroyed, he gets back on his feet and comes for you.

The same truism applies to human beings. Many are the good guys who've shot the bad guy dead center, watched him crash into the furniture Hollywood-style, holstered their weapon, turned and walked away, only to catch a bullet in the back of the head.

These are things you learn at Gunsite too—at least you do if Louis Awerbuck is instructing.

So, a week and a lifetime after you enter the raven gates of Gunsite, you leave. But you're likely to find that sometime during that week in the country, your DNA shifted and recomposed in some subtle way that you didn't notice. The world you are now reentering is not quite the same world it was just a few days ago. Something has happened, either to the world or to you, and nothing will ever be quite the same again. You feel you've left something behind at Gunsite. And the odds are, you'll be back.

Gunsite Academy
Paulden, AZ
www.gunsite.com

# Ravings of a Madman

## Louis Awerbuck

8

**L**ouis Awerbuck is perfectly sane. Anyone who has carried, used, and taught the 1911 for as long as this man has can't be otherwise.

Awerbuck's clarity of mind is one of the many reasons he stands out from the crowd in these crazy times. The way he works a class in defensive pistol, whether at Gunsite or any number of other training centers around the country and under the auspices of his own Yavapai Firearms Academy, renews your faith that there are indeed true and dedicated teachers whose only interest is imparting life-saving knowledge to their students. Awerbuck is renowned for his advanced courses in pistol, rifle, shotgun, and subgun, with the emphasis on strategies and tactics. Jeff Cooper once told me that he considers Awerbuck one of the top half dozen firearms instructors in the world. With Cooper's help, Awerbuck immigrated to the United States from his native South Africa 20 years ago and has been instructing high-level firearms classes full time ever since.

Awerbuck is not the only gifted firearms instructor on the planet. It's a given that Jeff Cooper himself was a brilliant teacher when he was still taking students. Clint Smith of Thunder Ranch is said to be such a man. I know from personal experience that Max Joseph of TFTT is an instructor of the very highest order. The pistol each of these masters of the art of pistolcraft has carried constantly for decades, used as a pistol is meant to be used, and taught to the best of their extraordinary abilities is John Browning's 1911. Just in case you were wondering.

There are undoubtedly a few more good firearms instructors around, but not a hell of a lot. The general level of instruction you get at the thousands of firearms academies that have sprouted up around the country during the last few

Louis Awerbuck, says Jeff Cooper, is one of the top half dozen firearms instructors in the world. Awerbuck and the author met for dinner at the Little Thumb Butte Bed & Breakfast just a couple miles from Gunsite in Chino Valley, Arizona. The discussion centered on the psychology of defensive handgunning. Photo by the author.

years is probably adequate for students seeking to improve their mechanical shooting skills, but few of these schools can offer the life-changing experience a serious shooter can get from the best born instructors.

After spending a recent week watching Awerbuck work during a defensive pistol class, I wanted to get him off the range for a few hours and ask him some questions. We met for dinner a few miles from Gunsite at the Little Thumb Butte Bed & Breakfast, a favorite retreat for Gunsite students, where owner and hostess Ann Harrington served us a wonderful home-cooked meal on a private balcony overlooking endless juniper-dotted hills with a river running through them.

Among his other personality attributes, Louis Awerbuck is a very humble guy. If there is a gulf between the way he thinks and the behavior and attitude of society in general, Awerbuck is quick

to admit that maybe he's the one who's crazy. Let's hope this is his sense of humor speaking. In any case, the title of this interview was his idea. And Louis Awerbuck is not a man you're too tempted to argue with.

I asked Awerbuck what was the toughest thing to teach people about shooting.

"For beginners, it's probably realizing it's easier than they think it is. They tend to overthink the problem," he said. "For experienced people, trying to correct ingrained problems they've had for years. That's much harder."

**Q: A lot of guys can teach the mechanics, which is fairly simple, don't you think?**

A: It is extremely simple. It's sights, trigger, follow-through. That's all it is; that's all it ever has been. Once the firing grip, the stance, the shooting platform, and that type of thing are worked out. The actual operation of sending a projectile downrange on a steady target is sights, trigger, follow-through. Most people try to shoot too accurately and overthink the problem. They

"The actual operation of sending a projectile downrange on a steady target is sights, trigger, follow-through. Most people overthink the problem." Photo by the author.

try for 110 percent and wind up with 40 percent. My draw to the game is the psychology of it, the whys and wherefores. It always has been.

**Q: I just read your book *Tactical Reality*, and you talk a lot about that. I especially liked your chapters dealing with heart and mind. That's a pretty deep subject.**

A: It's real deep for a young kid. But none of this is new. This stuff is 5,000 years old. It's the same mind-set as the samurai, the ninja, Genghis Khan, the Romans, the Greeks, the Spanish—you can just keep on going back through the ages. It was always the same thing.

**Q: Why do some people not get it?**

A: Some of the people who don't get it are highly skilled professional people—like a commercial pilot, a neurosurgeon, somebody who cannot afford to make the slightest slip in his normal occupation, so he overthinks every single thing when he's firing a weapon or taking his pistol from the holster. They'll "what if" things to death.

Other people who don't get it are not really fighting oriented. From what I've seen, I think it's

"People tend to think that if you pay a certain amount of money to be taught how to do something with a firearm, the net result at the end of the day is that you will be able to do it. It's like paying to have your brakes fixed." Photo by the author.

a societal thing. Let's face it, in North America you can pretty much buy anything you want. So people tend to think that if you pay a certain amount of money to be taught how to do something with a firearm, the net result at the end of the day is that you will be able to do it. It's like paying to have your brakes fixed or paying for an appendectomy. They're paying for a service, and they expect it to be done. They don't figure they need any ability themselves or that they're going to have to put some of themselves into it.

I get civilian classes, especially in California, with a large Oriental clientele. You can see the difference in the mind-set straightaway. A lot sharper, a lot stronger, a lot more fighting oriented, and deeper thinkers. You can see it on the first day of a level-one pistol class. Most of them are not more than second-generation, so there's a survival thing. Somebody scrabbled and did laundry for 80 years on a back street in Hong

"My draw to the game is the psychology of it, the whys and wherefores. It always has been." Photo by the author.

Kong to get enough food on the table so that the first one could finally go to school, to college, to America, or whatever. They've kept that traditional mind-set, and it transfers over to guns on a firing range. Samoans—all of them are fighters. Every one of them. Why would a Samoan who's been in this country 30 years be a good fighter? His mind-set is stable.

**Q: What do the nonwarriors do when they get in trouble?**

A: They will probably have their pistol taken away, because really and truly, deep down inside they are not prepared to take life, even in defense of their own. So they'll probably have their pistol taken away, get shot with their own pistol, and then the crook will leave with their pistol and shoot another person with it.

**Q: A lot of instructors have told me the toughest problem they have to deal with is that something like 80 percent of people are not capable of shooting another person.**

A: If a shooter cannot look somebody in the eye at six feet and be prepared to take a human life, he shouldn't be carrying a gun. A lot of people think they're prepared to do it; they can whack Bambi in the Coconino Forest. But when it comes to looking a human—who just happens to be an animal walking on his back legs—in the eyes and delivering rounds, they can't do it. You would think it would be a hell of a lot easier to shoot a human who's running toward you with a Bowie knife than a deer who's running away.

I think it's a function of being dumbed down as a society. My God, somebody's about to shoot and kill me, let me get on the cell phone and call 911. Law enforcement will magically materialize and interject themselves between me and this guy 6 feet away who's coming into me with a 12-inch knife. They don't reach for a 1911. They pick up the phone and call 911. Even after they saw 9/11 happening on the TV set in their living rooms.

It's the noise in your car engine. If I turn the radio up, the noise in the engine goes away. No it doesn't. That motor's going to blow up. Get the engine fixed now or you're going to be stranded on the side of the highway with your fancy radio. Every silver lining has a dark cloud. I'm not a pessimist, I'm a realist.

"If a shooter cannot look somebody in the eye at six feet away and be prepared to take a human life, he shouldn't be carrying a gun." Photo by the author.

**Q: Do you see a certain parallel between defensive pistol shooting and dangerous-game hunting?**

A: Sure, as far as the adrenal dump, the chemical cocktail. Bambi is just pipes, wires, meat, bone, gristle, blood, the same as the rapist in the back alley.

**Q: But I'm talking about dangerous game. The hunter is not afraid of Bambi. Dangerous game is more like the guy running toward you with the Bowie knife.**

A: If I'm afraid of you, in fear of my life, I need to do something about it. But we've grown up in a society where other people protect us. We expect to make a phone call and somebody will be there. It's like pulling the blanket over your head to protect yourself from the bogeyman.

**Q: That reminds me of the story about a cop who draws his gun and empties it into the floor so the bad guy won't take it away from him. What's going on there?**

A: If you're talking of the same real-life incident I'm thinking of, that was a gunfight from hell. The cop and his partner went to serve a summons, and this guy had had a problem with his wife the night before or got out of bed on the wrong side or something, and as soon as the two cops walked in he grabbed the woman officer's gun and killed her with it, right off the bat. So then this gunfight from hell ensued. The officer wound up with two guns, both revolvers. And he drained one into the floor of the house so this guy couldn't take it and use it on him while he was trying to reload the other one. He reloaded twice, in one room, in a gunfight; it went on for nearly two minutes. He shot the guy through the rib cage, contact work. The guy dropped, and then he got up when the officer turned around. The guy got up and hit the cop with a two-by-four.

The thing is, in a gunfight you don't know what you've done afterwards, retrospectively. You think you know what you've done; you'll backtrack everything to the premise to which you want to backtrack it. It's got four wheels and it's a Chevy, therefore my truck's a Chevy because it has four wheels, even though it's a Ford. You can backtrack anything to a premise.

It's like if you advocate what's colloquially called point shooting and you tag somebody—you're in a deadly force situation, and you fire one round and hit him right between the eyes at 30 feet. You are going to convince yourself that you point-shot that round. You may have used sighted fire. You don't know.

Col. David Hackworth had a real good expression to the effect that your perception in battle is only as wide as your battle sights. If you take five people involved in one incident and separate them straight after the incident, you'll get five different stories of what happened. We have no perception of what's happening when it's happening. I've seen a guy with a bolt rifle drain four rounds out of it, just running the bolt, never pressing the trigger, not understanding why the springbok didn't fall over. There are people with a semiautomatic pistol in a fight who never press the trigger, run the slide, never press the trigger, run the slide and jack out 8 or 14 live rounds on the floor. It's called buck fever. That fascinates me. It's the psychology; it's all mental.

I'm not God's gift to shooting, but what does it take to hit a target? A static range target. Sights, trigger, follow-through. So why do you go out there and shoot 10 rounds and miss after 40 years and Lord knows how many millions of rounds? Something goes askew in your head; you just do something stupid like yank on the trigger or fail to follow through with the sights.

There is nothing to taking a neophyte and teaching him how to shoot. The best-shooting pistol class you will ever see is a dozen 14-year-old females who have never touched a pistol. Are they gunfighters? I don't know, but as far as mechanical shooting goes you can't ask for anything more. A class of 14-year-old females will turn out amazing pistol shooters. They don't have an ego, they haven't got the prior mistakes (even in this day and age, it's usually the son who gets taken out to shoot by daddy), so they don't know how to miss.

**Q: Shooting under pressure—training or competition—is as close as we can get to real life. Why does that pressure clarify and speed up the minds of some people but scramble the brains of others?**

A: Everybody has a button. The bottom line is, you cannot put pressure on me if I don't allow you to do it. If I want to subjugate myself mentally to allow you to do something to me on a range that will affect the basic mechanical operation of what I always do, then I'm going to scramble my brain. If you give me a drill, the drill sinks in, and I understand what the drill is, and I churn it out, that's what Gunnie [Carlos] Hathcock called "getting in the bubble."

Jeff [Cooper]'s "Flying M" [a man-on-man shoot-off drill] is still being used today. I don't know when he first used it, but I've been with him 25 years, so I know it's been around a quarter century. Every Friday afternoon in a 250 [defensive pistol] class at Gunsite, you have one so-called winner who's usually pretty good, and the rest are "also-rans." But you don't really have a winner; you have people who beat themselves over and over. The winner of the Flying M is hardly ever somebody who was better than three-quarters of the class; he just kept his feces coagulated, that's all he did. It's a three-round draw—bang, bang, speed load, bang. That's all it is. It's something 95 percent of the people in the class are capable of doing Wednesday afternoon. But at the end of the class, there's a needle in the head. It's all a mind deal.

Everybody keeps saying the gun is just a tool. The bottom line is, the gun is just a tool. It really

"Everybody keeps saying the gun is just a tool. The bottom line is, the gun is just a tool." Photo by the author.

is. It's a piece of metal. How many times are you going to let a two-pound piece of metal outwit you? We're not talking about flying a Tomcat here; this is not brain surgery. But it is psychology.

**Q: Do you still get a kick out of instructing?**

A: Absolutely. Otherwise I wouldn't be doing it. If I'd wanted to make money in my life, I would have done something else. Because you can't do this job right and make a fortune out of it. You can make a good living, be comfortable, you can eat and have a roof over your head. But if you're making a fortune in money you're putting the money as a priority, and I have a moral and ethical problem with that. I'm not saying I'm the world's altruist. But if you make money your priority, or ego your priority, you've got a problem. And there's lot of that. It's become rampant in this game in the last 10 years.

**Q: Why the last 10 years especially?**

A: I have a theory; it's a personal theory. It's probably wrong. Once concealed carry came out, pretty much anybody could teach it. You're teaching it out of a book; it's primarily law. You go to Gunsite or Thunder Ranch or Blackwater or any of the big-name schools, you take a class as a student, and all of a sudden you open your own school and you're a firearms instructor.

To decide that you know everything about firearms and tactics is about the most pompous thing you can do. A doctor's got to go to university; an auto mechanic is going to be out of work if he doesn't get updated training on all this technology in cars today. A weapons instructor just says, "Hi, I'm a weapons instructor, and I know all about guns and training and tactics and strategy." And people pay their money. You look at instructor résumés, and they've taken all the classes, but what have they done? To give you the authority, what you've done is taken everybody else's lesson plans and put them into a program of your own and you're teaching it like a parrot.

**Q: There's definitely a proliferation of so-called firearms academies, some of them run by IPSC guys who win a couple of titles and open a school.**

A: IPSC guys are very good shooters. Obviously, IPSC has changed from the early days, from what Jeanne-Pierre Denis and Jeff [Cooper] and the original guys set out to make it. The P was meant to stand for practical. The arguments went on in the '80s and very early '90s about whether it's practical or it isn't. Finally, IPSC got to the stage in the early '90s where they said, "No, we're not being practical, it's a sport." But the bottom line is, if you get somebody like Rob Leatham, Jerry Barnhard, guys like that, they're tremendous mechanical shooters. And if they open a school and teach mechanical shooting, which a lot of them do, I think there's nothing wrong with that.

**Q: But is mechanical shooting what is needed by most people who get their concealed-carry permits and want to protect themselves?**

A: How many people who get concealed-carry permits do you think are serious about it? How many do you think want to punch a piece of paper so they can legally have a firearm if one day they might need it? Most people buy a gun, take a concealed-carry class, buy a box of 50 rounds of ammunition, and the firearm and 50 rounds of ammunition are found in their estate 30 years later. In a drawer somewhere.

**Q: Those people need to initiate a thought process more than they need to learn how to shoot well.**

A: I pulled a pendulum clock apart once, stripped the entire thing down and couldn't get it back together again. Don't you think that a clockmaker would have said, why is this guy pulling this clock apart? Like we're saying, why is this guy carrying a gun, why isn't he serious, why didn't he go through a thought process? With us it's firearms strategy and tactics; with somebody else it's a clock.

The only difference is, survival is instinctual. It's not a learned habit. And these days something strange is happening. Look at a 13- or 14-year-old kid today. He was raised in a world of political correctness—not hitting back, turning the other cheek. He's lost his self-protective instinct. Look at 9/11. People said, "This is terrible, somebody's bombed these buildings, this is absolutely horrific, somebody needs to do something about it." Who somebody? I don't know because I can't do it, I'm busy right now. Self-preservation is being bred out of us. It's cyclical. Every 100, 200 years it happens. Today, if somebody has a power failure for an hour you'll get stampeded to death at Safeway for a run on candles. You can't last an hour in the dark in your own house.

War has always been the solution. War has always solved all the problems. You reduce the number of mouths to feed. Everybody's got a job. Instincts are reinvigorated. That's why there's continuous war. When man actually lit the first fire and figured out how flame works, he said, "Now who can we go burn?"

And the world is getting smaller, no question, because of technology. At an amazing pace. We're losing the ability to think. Do we need the ability to think? Right now, yes, but we may not in 40 years' time. Once technology is perfected, you may not have to think for yourself. If you're in a car that drives itself to work on a GPS and your grandkids are going to the moon for a weekend vacation . . .

**Q: So why do a growing number of people still think they need to learn to shoot?**

A: Because the gun still represents the equality of power. Whether it's a little old lady from Pasadena or a muscle man, with a gun they can deliver equal power from a distance, whether 6 feet or 60 yards. Some people are realizing the glory days are gone. The world is pretty much hell-bent for destruction. We're in for a worldwide religious war from hell that is going to make the other world wars look like Sunday picnics. Right now you have laws: you can't carry a gun here, you can't do this there, you can't spit on the sidewalk. These may be fine in a peaceful society. But when you've got a society that's gone mad, worldwide, the law of the jungle supersedes all other laws.

Look at the year 2000, when the world was supposed to be coming to an end. It could have, for all that I knew. You had people hoarding stuff and then standing on the TV smiling at the camera and pointing to their house with their address on the front door. Proudly displaying their two years' worth of life-saving food and water when they're not capable of lasting two hours in their own house with the lights off. That's part of what it is, buying something material like a gun as a symbolic way of protecting themselves.

**Q: Are pop culture and the mass media leading this or following it?**

A: I think it's self-feeding. When I first came out here there were all the standing jokes about the *National Enquirer,* but the national media is pretty much the same as the *National Enquirer* now. The media is a lot to blame, but if people are going to blame the media and it's self-feeding and you're going to buy this to read it, of course they're going to give you what you want. If there's no market, there's no seller. It's like drugs. You can bomb Colombia till it's a parking lot, but if you don't stop the person in Phoenix, Arizona, from snorting the stuff up his nose there will be a market. Somebody will make the stuff. If the person in Phoenix doesn't snort the stuff up his nose there is no market, there is no point in manufacturing it because you can't sell it to anybody because nobody wants it. It's as plain and simple as that. Supply and demand.

**Q: You wouldn't think this country would have got so soft so quickly, would you?**

A: You would and you wouldn't. Something like 9/11, yeah it's a tragedy, but it's not like this is the first time something like this has ever happened in the history of the world. People over here wonder why somebody sitting in South Africa or Germany may ask, Well, what have we been saying for 30 years? What are you getting so excited about? It's a tragedy, absolutely it's a tragedy, but all of a sudden now it's a worldwide problem. It's been a worldwide problem for 30 or 40 years. Everybody's been telling us that, but it's been so warm and cozy here. Now we say we've got to do something about it, we need to call somebody.

I have a buddy in California whose daughter's boyfriend just got suspended from school. In California it's a big deal to get suspended from school. With all their political correctness, you've just about got to murder somebody. This kid is a really good kid. By today's standards, it's almost bizarre what a good kid he is. The reason he was suspended is because he grabbed another kid by the shoulder and told him to cut it out because that kid was walking around the school grabbing girls' boobs from behind. So, for doing what clearly needed to be done, he was suspended.

I love dogs, but if one comes here and he's jumping at me with all his teeth showing and white foam around his mouth, he hasn't just been brushing his teeth with Crest. He's rabid. As much as I love dogs, I'm going to have to kill him. The problem is people standing there saying, "Maybe he's just a clever dog who can brush his own teeth and forgot to rinse his mouth." And then they'll start discussing 15 brands of toothpaste. They just miss the point entirely.

**Q: You're the only guy I know who carries both a 1911 and a Glock.**

A: I've got my reasons. The 1911 was made as a fighting weapon, and it works. I don't want extraneous levers and things on my weapons. The little Glock 19 I carry as a backup works too. Your so-called backup gun is really an alternate weapon because you may not be able to get to the primary. Using different weapons is just mind-set. I've always carried a 1911 as my primary weapon, and I used to run a .44 Special revolver as a backup until I changed to the Glock.

I firmly believe a .45 is better than a .44 1/2, and I think a Tomcat fighter jet is better than a

shotgun. Unfortunately, I can't get a Tomcat or a shotgun in a holster, so rule number one is to hit your target. It does no good to miss the target, but people are missing. The .45's been out for 150 years if you include the British Webleys. They've always got the job done.

The sorry truth is, my brother got killed with one round from a .32 S&W revolver. Stone dead. It hit him in the head, and he's dead. No matter what you carry, your primary objective is hitting the target. You cannot turn a handgun into a big-game rifle; I don't care what you do to it. And if you did, it would be unmanageable in a gunfight. So people are not hitting the target, and it comes back to training.

I've got a problem with flat targets, nonrepresentative street or battle targets. We're talking about shooting people, and if the target is an 18 x 30-inch piece of flat paper, this has nothing to do with reality. All males from the shoulder line to the waist are the same height, whether it's me or a basketball player. And from nipple to nipple they're all nine inches wide. So in a full frontal shot, if you're out nine inches you've got nothing. And if people are going to be kind enough to stand like that, why are you shooting them? They're probably twisted in like this with an AK or a blade and you're down to three or four inches of target.

But you've got to start somewhere. If you've got a neophyte you've got to teach him the basics. The problem is, what is an advanced gunfight? There is no advanced gunfight. I'm running with curved targets, graphic targets, angled this way and that and everything else. But you've got to start somebody off with flat paper, explain this is the trigger, these are the sights, this is the follow-through, get him to shoot a group on a piece of paper. You can get an organ grinder's monkey to shoot a group on a piece of paper; he can take his paw and pull the trigger back, and he can shoot accurately. That's all there is to it. Has this got anything to do with shooting people, when the target is that big and three feet away from you and is about to turn you into a little brown shit spot on the ground?

People are very, very hard to hit because a lot of shooters cannot transpose the angles of a biped to a quadruped. You were talking about dangerous game earlier on. What comes at you like a human? Maybe a polar bear, that's about it. Everything else runs on four legs, but a human is usually on his hind paws most of the time when you have this problem. People have trouble transposing this concept into a vertical instead of a horizontal problem. I bend one piece of cardboard, splice it with another, and then staple a target over that, then I angle them some way or twist them or turn them. Now you've got to start thinking about going into the rib cage, side of the head, simulating a fight on stairs. If the guy is lying in a bed, say the head's facing you and the feet are away, you have to go in real high, because if you shoot at the chest and miss by five degrees you're going to miss him entirely.

**Q: Do you teach outside the States much these days?**

A: Not a lot. I go to Switzerland next year. I won't do South America, and there are some very good people in South America. The problem is, I live in the United States, and the United States vacillates every four or five years between friend and enemy, and I do not want to be Ollie North four years later. I'll do Switzerland next year, but I can't remember the last time we had a war with Switzerland.

Plus my schedule. I'm 56 years old, and I'm still running 10 1/2 or 11 months of the year flat out on the road. Since I last talked to you a few weeks ago I've been in practically every town in California. Do I need to go on a world tour right now? No. Plus the airlines are a pain in the rear. To fly to Germany for a three-day class and have to deal with the hassles of international customs and the airlines is not worth it.

And I don't like working without my own target systems. I do not run with flat targets after the first day of the class. You can't correlate them to a human antagonist problem. Nobody looks like a nonmoving IPSC target. Nobody. With all due deference to Mr. Pepper, I don't use Pepper poppers because they're too easy. The full-size Pepper popper is 42 inches high and pretty wide. You can hit it in the knees or the top of the skull, and it falls over. They're too easy to hit. I'd rather use irregularly shaped steel. Not square. If you take a steel target that's 10 inches square, do you think that if it were 10 inches in diameter circular, the same amount of people would hit it the same amount of times? The last time I saw square people, they were all dead.

I made a decision when I started training, from all the people from whom I'd learned and the one or two things I'd seen in my life, that range targets were not representative of the street. That's the first thing I changed. I use humanoid targets (or, as I was told in California, you've got to use the word *anthropomorphic*) with lateral angles, irregular three-dimensional shapes with erratic movement. I soon found out that people who could shoot great groups at 20 yards would miss these at 10 feet with shots going all over the place.

A hundred years ago, nobody missed. Because they had one round for the family's musket and daddy told you to get your 12-year-old butt out there and go fetch lunch, and if you came back without lunch, where's the ball and where's the powder? Jeff Cooper rehammered this into people's heads, he's still doing it, and I don't think enough credit is being given to him. That annoys me. Everything I know that my dad didn't teach me, Jeff Cooper did. They were my two mentors. Jeff's definition of a marksman is somebody who can hit his target, whatever that target may be, on demand, right now.

**Q: What are you going to do when you retire?**

A: I will probably not retire. And if I did, I would stay in some aspect of the game. I've got a metabolism from hell, I can run 24 hours a day, and I'm quick for my age, though I obviously don't have my 22-year-old reactions. I'll know it before anybody else, but when my reactions slow down to where I miss your hand when I'm grabbing for it, I'll quit the next day because I'd be running an unsafe range. I don't want to sound supercilious, but I'm getting like the humble martial artist who finally realizes that he needs another 400 years of this. I'm at base level—I've finally got a little bit of knowledge; now I've got to start climbing the tree.

Louis Awerbuck
Yavapai Firearms Academy
Prescott Valley, AZ
www.yfainc.com

# Safety and
# Survival

9

A 1911 pistol, whether it's a .45 or a 9mm or a .22, is not something you want to drop the hammer on when the muzzle is pointed at anything you really don't want to destroy beyond recognition. Gun safety rules are simple, easy to learn, easy to follow, and guaranteed to keep you and those around you alive for a little while longer. Unfortunately, gun safety rules are also easy to break. Even if you're not some kind of congenital airhead. The penalty for such momentary stupidity and negligence is immediate, absolute, and irrevocable. Final disposition nonnegotiable, apologies not accepted. If you don't blow your own brains out, you may well wish you had.

A young Cape buffalo bull will often leave the large matriarchal herd in which he has been raised and in which he has as yet little part to play, and go off to hang out with a male-only group of solitary-minded old bachelor bulls that have been around the horn, so to speak. The old bulls spend their days bathing in riverine mud, dozing in the shade, and grumbling to each other about the stupidity of a society dominated by a bunch of fat, old, overmothering cows with scraggly hair between their skinny horns. If the old bulls allow the young one to stay for a while, it's because they know he's ready to learn something about safety and survival in a world where you never know when you might run into a pride of hungry lions or a tourist with a .577 Nitro Express over his shoulder.

The young bull never questions the wisdom of the old ones. This is what allows him to live long enough to rejoin the herd, have fun with the girls for a little while, and gather enough ugly scars from his brothers to make him a good trophy before he grows cynical and solitary enough to pick up and move on down by the river himself.

If a student questions his teachers, thereby breaking the flow of information, he must then be prepared to teach himself. Most students aren't, at least in the early stages of education, and therefore place their entire trust in the person who professes to know a lot more than they do. This is both good and bad. Good because it allows a quantity of information to be transferred efficiently. Bad because there aren't many teachers who are anywhere near as smart or as honest as a Cape buffalo bull. Just look at the politicized agenda that passes for a college curriculum these days.

The thread that connects teachers and students is a fragile one, and it may be easily broken by any of the participants at any time with a variety of consequences.

The following actually happened:

It was about halfway through a combat pistol class at a good school. The class was on the young side, fully attentive, and remarkably free of obvious knuckleheads and jackasses, except for one sort of bigmouth retired cop who had been ridiculing the course and the instructors out of the side of his mouth for days. After a somewhat sloppy drill, one of the instructors had a word with the class. Being a no-nonsense kind of guy, the instructor did not talk to them like babies but reminded the students that they were not concentrating nearly as hard as they could and asked them to pay closer attention and to think of this drill not as an exercise in paper-punching but as a gunfight. He presented his point well, obviously injecting an extra measure of motivation in the students who were slowing down in the afternoon heat. A good lesson for those who were there to learn.

The retired cop, by this time known by many in the class as Mr. Dickhead, was apparently not there to learn and took great exception to being dressed down as part of the group. Hands on hips like a little girl, he had a tantrum, exploding in an uncontrolled emotional display and yelling obscenity after obscenity at the instructor.

Must be a joke, everyone thought. Surely the retired cop had too much experience to break down and blow up over nothing, to launch an irrational attack on the respect the other students had given

to this instructor, whose potentially life-saving advice they had been listening to intently. Who could seriously be that stupid and unstable and disrespectful to everybody on the range?

But Mr. Dickhead was not joking, and he continued to carry on like a really badly spoiled child until everyone in class was ready to slap him hard upside the head and shove a dirty sock in his mouth. Many of the students wondered why the lead instructor didn't just tell him to shut up, pack his gear, and go home to his mama. But the lead instructor was a patient man, clearly used to dealing with assholes on occasion, and he had a private chat with this one, after which the man's volubility as well as his volume went down and everybody lived happily ever after.

Well, not quite everybody.

No one got the word until the next morning, but something had happened during the night, a few hours after what became known as Mr. Dickhead's Holiday in LaLa Land, that served to illustrate the prime, nonnegotiable, classic, number one firearms safety rule in the most powerful way imaginable.

Two friends were taking the course together, doing as well as you might expect from less experienced shooters. After class, they went out to dinner, joined by a third student who later said in sworn testimony that not a drop of alcohol had been consumed in his presence. After dinner, the two friends retired to the local hotel where they were staying. The scenario that followed, according to evidence pieced together by police and prosecutors, went something like this: The two guys, best friends since high school, one now with wife and kids, decided to spend a few minutes practicing their draw and dry-firing. Not in front of the usual full-length hotel-room mirror, famous for being death on the traveling salesman straightening his tie or the lady taking her dress off in the next room; they knew that much. So, trusting each other implicitly, they got it into their heads to stand across the small room from each other and face off Hollywood style.

What you think happened, happened. One very loud gunshot rang out and one of the two best friends lay dead on the floor, his chest blown out by a .45 slug.

"Don't worry, it's not loaded." Photo by Daniel P. Gresham, 1973–2004.

Whether Mr. Dickhead's Holiday In LaLa Land and the Shootout at The Best Friends' Hotel were connected in any way, by anything other than a simple coincidence of time, nobody will ever know. The deadly recklessness that may lie just beneath the surface of an apparently rational person is not something anybody can see.

Two things are certain: One, the firearms teaching environment is highly sensitive, extremely intense, and, for lack of a stronger way to put it, not to be fucked with by self-absorbed nitwits. Two, the very last thing in the world you ever want to do is shoot somebody out of negligence.

These are not things you learn in established herds of females and adolescents, despite all their restrictive rules and regulations. These are things you learn from the scarred-up old bulls down by the river.

It has always amazed me how many people—including a lot of those who have grown up around guns but have had no formal training, including some serious and even professional hunters, including at least half of the mental giants who have memorized each and every one of the safety rules and can parrot them back on command—handle guns in ways that can kill you.

Such careless shooters have not taken a moment to actually train themselves in safe gun handling, which is a skill set unto itself. They have not even attempted to engrave the proper handling of firearms into their psyches. These self-centered, slipshod so-called shooters simply have no respect for the people around them. Their offended response when they see you staring at them is always, "It's not loaded," and they expect you to accept their word without question.

The point is not that a particular gun is in fact safe under a certain set of circumstances but that these people are practicing and ingraining habits that will not be safe with a different gun under different circumstances. If they wave the muzzle of an unloaded gun around, they will wave the muzzle of a loaded gun around. If they rest their finger in the trigger guard when they're pointing the gun downrange, one day they'll rest their finger in the trigger guard when they're pointing the gun in your direction. If they hold the gun up to the side of their head to lower the hammer on an empty chamber, one day they will, hopefully, blow their own eardrum out instead of yours.

It has been my observation that, as a general rule, people who have been trained in combat pistol shooting tend to be safer than most other shooters. Maybe it's because the short muzzle of a pistol demands more thought to control than the long muzzle of a rifle or a shotgun. Maybe it's because they're used to having other armed people around at close range. Maybe it's because they have at least had some training, which most rifle and shotgun shooters have not. There are obvious exceptions to the general rule.

I don't know what the killer at The Best Friends' Hotel said to the police, but it was surely some variation of the contemptible old refrain, "I didn't know the gun was loaded."

Remember this: your 1911 is *always* loaded. And just as deadly efficient as the day John Browning designed it to kill the enemies of your country.

# Muzzle Flashes of Insight

## 10

Original thoughts do not arise in an abstract intellectual vacuum, which explains why the academic mind is such a feeble instrument. Revealing insights occur only when you drop the hammer on a live round in the real world. Or, sometimes, when you sit down and talk with somebody who makes a living doing that.

## A WELL-USED SPRINGFIELD

When I first met Max Joseph going on 15 years ago, he had a Springfield Armory 1911A1 on his hip. At the time, Max was running an advanced weapons class for civilians. He was also running similar programs for the military and law enforcement, providing high-level VIP protection for a few clients, and competing in national three-gun matches. Since then, Max's reputation as an instructor and resulting high-intensity training assignments have taken him all over the world and allowed him to produce some of the best professional shooters ever to face the guns of the bad guys.

Resting on Max's hip today is that same Springfield Armory 1911A1. It's had a lot of rounds through it since I first saw it. The finish is a little more worn. There's a little more authority in the rattle of its slide against the frame. Max finally added an ambidextrous thumb safety because he's left-handed, though he had no trouble at all operating the right-handed Springfield before that little luxury was added. It's still smacking down steel targets, and God only knows what else it has been called upon to smack down in its half-hidden career.

Max has strong feelings about the 1911:

Max Joseph's 5-year-old son Paul doesn't have the form yet, but he's got the heart. Under the personal tutelage of one of the world's best firearms instructors, who just happens to be his father, it won't be long before he has it all, probably including this well-used Springfield. Photo by Max Joseph.

The 1911 is close to my heart. I have carried that weapon with me as my primary personal defense pistol for the last 22 years. It's the perfect weapon for men that are going to master it. Without a doubt, a 1911 in the hands of a competent operator is the finest fighting handgun ever designed by mankind. The trouble is, most of the people who carry it do not and will not spend the time to master it. I pull my hair out at guys who carry a 1911 and won't use it properly. They won't ride their safety high, they continually get all these customizations done that make their guns malfunction. I'm tired of yelling at men that are spending $3,000 for a .45 and they're having stoppages with it. Too many people attempt to substitute skill with technology.

The reason my Springfield keeps banging away is because I've had just the most Spartan work done to it, didn't have any tightening done, I wanted it to be loose like Browning designed it so it keeps functioning with dirt and mud and sand.

I remember the first time I held a 1911. My brother was in the Merchant Marines and he came home when I was about 8 or 9 years old and he showed me his .45, a straight old government-surplus .45. He unloaded it and let me hold it. Then he put it back in his suitcase and told me not to touch it. As soon as he left the house to go out with his buddies, I went straight to that suitcase, took out his .45, unloaded it, and started taking it apart. Right away, of course, the plunger spring shot out of it and I couldn't figure out how to put it back together. I just slid the recoil spring back and stuck the plunger in but I didn't rotate the bushing. I put the gun back in his suitcase thinking he would never notice. My brother pulled me out of bed about midnight that night and taught me a lesson about messing with somebody else's .45. He still has that gun, but I haven't played with it in quite some time.

One reason why quality operators prefer the 1911 is the way the pistol feels in your hand while it's firing, the way the weapon recoils. The controllability is excellent and allows for very rapid sight reacquisition and follow-up. I find that many other models of pistols in .45 and even some .40 and, believe it or not, even some models of 9mm recoil sharper and in a less uniform fashion. The 1911 doesn't bark in your hand, it just rolls in your hand when it recoils. And that really is a very, very good feeling.

When some young student asks me why I carry a 1911, here's what I tell them: LAPD has 9,000 officers and they all carry Berettas or Smith & Wessons. LAPD SWAT kills people on a weekly basis and they all carry 1911s. Single-stack 1911s, not Para-Ordnance and all the hybrid stuff. The U.S. Marine Corps carries Berettas, but Marine Corps Recon carries single-stack 1911s. The entire army went to Berettas, but

If this Springfield could talk . . . Photo courtesy of TFTT.

If your first impression of Position Sul is that it looks funny, you're not alone. Clint Smith once wrote some harsh words about Sul before he had properly evaluated it. He quickly followed up with a profuse apology for popping off about something he did not understand without knowing what he was talking about. Control yourself, Clint. Photo courtesy of TFTT.

Max has used this Springfield Armory 1911A1 for military, law enforcement, and civilian instruction, VIP protection, competition, and God knows what else for more than 15 years. Photo courtesy of TFTT.

Delta Force carries single-stack 1911s. There's something to that, you know. When you train guys up on a 1911, that weapon is unsurpassed. It's hard to explain. It's like a Harley-Davidson.

## THE READY POSITION GOES SOUTH

Max Joseph has been running TFTT for many years at such a high level that his school has earned a worldwide reputation among the most knowledgeable of shooters. Max has also worked for many years with longtime friend and associate Alan Brosnan as senior instructor for TEES (Tactical Explosive Entry School), which has also earned an international reputation of the highest order.

Some time ago, Joseph and Brosnan developed a revolutionary new ready position, which is being taught at both TFTT and TEES and is rapidly becoming the standard for high-speed team operators around the world. It rarely happens in the necessarily conservative world of firearms training that a new technique proves clearly and consistently superior to an established technique and is thus adopted by seasoned and highly skeptical instructors and intensively trained operators for use in life-and-death situations. When such a thing happens, it's always worthy of note.

Position Sul, developed by Max Joseph and Alan Brosnan, provides safer and more positive muzzle control along with a faster transition to the firing position than the low-, high- and horizontal-ready positions previously taught to individual members of high-speed team operations involving close-quarters work. *Sul* means south in Portuguese, and I've found the position to be as simple and elegant as it sounds.

Here's what Max Joseph has to say about it:

The importance of weapons control cannot be overstated. During any operation, we must always be 100 percent conscious of where our muzzle is directed. This is critical for the safety of ourselves, our team members, and any noncombatants. Ready positions of the past were developed on a square range, where all personnel are standing side-by-side in a straight line facing downrange. This is not the reality of working in a close, fast-paced operational environment.

SWAT trainers and combat instructors

have spent years cautioning personnel to watch their muzzles, but nobody thought to develop a ready position that better addresses the situation. Position Sul answers that problem.

Position Sul retains the weapon very close to the body for better control and retention in a crowded environment. It prevents a SWAT operator in a tight stack from covering the ass of the man in front of him, and it eliminates the tendency to project the weapon through doorways and around corners during entries. It's just a lot less rigid and more flexible.

An operator transitions to Position Sul from either low-ready or on-target. The elbows retract toward the body as the weapon begins rotating downward. The key is to keep the middle knuckle of the shooting hand in contact with the index finger of the weak hand. This is your index, or reference point, to your normal grip. The open palm of the nonshooting hand should be flat against the solar plexus. Elbows should be kept in close to the body to facilitate movement through tight areas. Of course, the trigger finger is always straight when the weapon is not on target.

The presentation from Sul to a proper shooting grip and sight plane is extremely fast, smooth, and natural. The technique offers a very natural "punch" method. This is where the weapon is tactically presented in a fashion that allows instant access of our sight plane without making our body unduly rigid or unstable. As the arms are extended toward the threat area, the weapon rotates toward the target, using the knuckle reference point. By the time the arms reach their extended position, the weapon should be locked into your normal grip.

One must remember that this position was developed for close quarters battle (CQB). CQB implies that suspects and possible hostages may be moving about in very tight quarters. While moving through doorways or down the crowded

passageways of an aircraft or bus, our weapon needs to be pulled in, close to our body, for purposes of weapon retention. The operators must be constantly aware of muzzle control for basic safety. The main benefit of Position Sul is that, when we are working with teammates, our ability to move together in close confines without violating muzzle control is greatly increased. Additionally, for training purposes, Position Sul allows a whole new array of drills to be executed safely— everything from stationary and moving turns to stacks on the door are much safer using this technique.

Max emphasized to me that there are only three situations when Position Sul should be used: (1) when you're in transit but *not* the cover man; (2) when friendlies are crossing in front of your arc of fire or located in your sphere of coverage; (3) when your job is the domination of crowds.

Position Sul ready position, developed by Max Joseph (shown here) and Alan Brosnan, is rapidly gaining acceptance and usage by high-intensity team operators from SWAT to SOG. Air Marshals, who currently use a horizontal ready position that covers the heads of passengers seated in the aircraft, are well advised to use Position Sul instead. Photo courtesy of TFTT.

Position Sul allows men to move safely in close quarters. While in Position Sul, the elbows are kept close in to the body. The key to fast acquisition is to keep contact between the middle knuckle of the shooting hand and the knuckle of the nonshooting index finger. The open palm of the nonshooting hand should be flat against the solar plexus. As the weapon is brought up, it is presented in a straight-line punch to the target. Photo courtesy of TFTT.

If you've ever sat in a first-class passenger seat up by the cockpit of an aircraft when an adrenaline-boosted air marshal was standing with his back to the cockpit door covering your head with the muzzle of his pistol in the horizontal-ready position, you'll appreciate one of the major benefits of Position Sul.

## THE RETURN OF ARMAND SWENSON

All my friends have lone-gunman-type personalities. Friendship, after all, requires something fundamental in common. If a man has no serious interest in guns and shooting, what could you possibly have to be friendly about? I don't have a single friend who counts himself as a football or basketball fan. All that tiresome cheerleading and tedious teamwork. I don't know any golfers. All that awkward motion and wasted time.

Interspecies friendships based on common interests are possible. Man and gundog. Man and racehorse. Man and his dangerous-game adversary. Maybe even man and trained monkey. But relationships with subhuman beasts can only go so far. For instance, I don't think friendship between man and Democrat is a possibility.

Besides guns, my friends have a wide variety of secondary interests, all of which are defined by great dollops of solitude, individual style, and flourish in environments of man-against-man, man-against-nature, man-against-himself, certainly not man-as-anonymous-socialist-unit.

Some of my lone-gunman friends are

occasional observers ("fan" is much too strong a word to describe their interest in watching other people's performances) of certain spectator sports, such as boxing (the one-on-one) or boxing-like big-time tennis (the singles game, not doubles). More are participants, whether in mountain climbing, chess, skydiving, esoteric martial arts, exploring a hidden bat cave, or sitting and smoking a good Cuban cigar. A few are cowboys and pool sharks. Those with a taste for speed, at least relative speed, and an appreciation for the beauty of line are passionate about airplanes, automobiles, and, most especially it seems, boats of both the wind-driven and engine-propelled variety.

Legendary 1911 gunsmith Armand Swenson was a boatman.

Speedboat racers know Swenson only as the designer and builder of a radical hydroplane boat-of-the-future. One of the most unusual boat designs in history, Swenson's hydroplane was powered by an aircraft engine and piloted by an automobile race driver. The boat's racing career was brief and disappointing, but Swenson's design innovations were so original that, 40 years after he built it in his own backyard, the boat was installed in the Seattle Hydroplane History Museum.

To gun-knowledgeable hunters, it was Armand Swenson's way with custom bolt-action hunting rifles that earned him acclaim, though he sought to keep his rifle-building business quiet for fear of being swamped. He liked solitude.

The talent that produced Swenson's greatest historical legacy, however, and with which his name is and will be associated more than any other, was his ability to coax the very best out of John Browning's 1911 pistol. Swenson was one of the earliest pioneers of that small group of talented gunsmiths dedicated to the big semiauto, and he was driven by an obsession for continuous improvements in accuracy, reliability, and handling. Swenson approached his job with the traditional tools of the custom gunsmith—refined craftsmanship, talented hands and eyes, and an unusual capacity for the design equivalent of dignified understatement. He had an appreciation for the beauty of line.

When Swenson's 1911s first attracted

nationwide attention, the term "racegun" had not yet been coined, nor had the bizarre design requirements yet been invented that would make the racegun about as useful on city streets as an open-wheeled race car. The leanings Swenson had toward the experimental, the radical, the interesting but impractical, he kept out of his gun work. That's what boats were for. Pistols, on the other hand, were serious business.

Swenson made 1911s that were accurate and reliable, in a time when many considered those two qualities mutually exclusive. He made 1911s that were good-looking and practical, pioneered better sights, developed the concept of melting the slide, and manufactured the first ambidextrous thumb safeties. He proved that you could chop and channel the big government .45 down to concealed-carry size without giving up absolutely reliable functioning. Otherwise, what would be the point? He built a lot of very beautiful guns, and he built a lot of them for cops, as practical a market as anyone could imagine.

Fellow gunsmith Terry Tussey, who was greatly influenced by Armand Swenson's body of work, sums up his success thusly: "Armand combined classic

Armand Swenson was concerned with improving the 1911 sight picture and often used rear sights from S&W K-frame revolvers to good effect. Photo courtesy of Wes Harms.

Unlike some of today's egocentric pistolsmiths, Armand Swenson signed his work discreetly. Photo courtesy of George Wester.

Swenson sometimes identified his guns with a simple S in a circle. Photo courtesy of George Wester.

Wayne Novak and Armand Swenson worked together for two years. This is one of the eight guns that bear both of their signatures. Note Swenson's characteristic squared-off trigger guard, the magazine well, and other subtle features. This circa 1981 Colt National Match with a Kart barrel was Novak's IPSC gun for several years. Photo courtesy of Wayne Novak.

This Swenson-Novak collaboration features a beveled mainspring housing, polished frame lines, and "the first ever hand-matted front strap," according to Wayne. Photo courtesy of Wayne Novak.

good looks with function . . . Armand always made form and function blend."

Famous sight maker Wayne Novak, back when he was just a kid, spent two years working for Swenson. He admits he can't begin to say how much he learned during those two years, but if you study Wayne's current custom guns closely you can sense the fighting spirit of Armand Swenson in them.

Today, there is again widespread agreement that the most desirable 1911 is an expertly refined version of the basic form-follows-function fighting gun. The quintessential Swenson touch, were it available from Swenson himself in this day and age, would undoubtedly be in the greatest possible demand. If you get lucky enough to find a vintage Swenson gun for sale, a rare occasion today, you'd better buy it before the line forming behind you gets restless. Because, as a well-known shooter said to me recently, "They don't make 'em like Armand Swenson anymore."

Well, maybe they don't and maybe they do.

I've seen some awfully good fighting 1911s built by some highly talented young pistolsmiths over the last few years—guns like Swenson would be building if he were still alive. It seems to me that the line of development from John Browning through extraordinary gunsmiths like Swenson to a few rising stars of today remains unbroken. There's just something about a 1911. The everlasting challenge of its near perfection will never cease to attract the highest new talents successive generations of gun makers can produce. You can bet your boat on it.

## DEVEL IN THE DETAILS

Charley Kelsey was one of that golden group of 1911 experimenters that included Swenson, Irv Stone Sr., Lee Jurras, Louis Seecamp, Wayne Novak, and quite a few others who showed the world the kinds of things that can be accomplished when generous measures of imagination and drive coalesce with a sound firearms design. Kelsey

Devel Socius .45 Colt Commander, with S&W adjustable rear sight, contoured mainspring housing, signature Devel trigger guard. Photo courtesy of Wayne Novak.

Charley Kelsey's personal Socius .38 Super, the most deluxe Devel ever made. Note the unusual grip safety. Photo courtesy of Wayne Novak.

Devel Gammon .45 made for Chip McCormick. Note long dust cover, flared magazine well. This is one of 21 Gammons ever made. Photo courtesy of Wayne Novak.

named his company Devel for an old Scottish word meaning to strike a swift and decisive blow, and he built guns accordingly. Kelsey built Smith & Wessons so well that he forced S&W to improve its own products and, with his engineering partner Wil Haupthoff, built 1911s that Colt should and would have built if there had been a brain in the boardroom. Kelsey also built some Devels that could only have been built by him.

Devel innovations were abundant, of both whimsical and highly practical varieties, and addressed nearly every fixed and working part of John Browning's gun. These included the signature hooked trigger guard; highly modified magazine wells and magazine releases; eight-round 1911 magazines; a totally new grip safety; a Swartz-type firing-pin block that worked off the hammer instead of the trigger, as in the disliked Series 80 Colt; a pivoting trigger; extreme free-

bored barrels; a patented bushingless conical barrel/slide lockup; new 9mm, 45-caliber, and 10mm cartridges; radical frangible and armor-piercing bullets; and a hell of a lot more.

Every Devel pistol is so distinctive it can be recognized on sight, and Wayne Novak of Novak Sights, one of Kelsey's original co-conspirators, has a fine collection of these highly creative and often highly efficient guns. They are all that remain to mark the colorful career of Charley Kelsey, whose professionally executed assassination in Texas in the spring of 2003 is a black political mystery that has yet to be solved.

## THE DETONICS DETONATIONS

One of the most interesting 1911s to come on the scene in the mid-'70s was the little Detonics CombatMaster. It was a very small, concealed-carry-size .45 in an era when only TV cops, movie assassins, and paperback novel heroes were popularly known to carry concealed handguns. The little gun had some pretty advanced features for the time, including a bulged barrel with no bushing, a multiple-spring recoil system with a guide rod, a lowered and scalloped ejection port, a polished feed ramp, and, best of all, a solid backstrap with no grip safety. According to several accounts, the frame and most other components were made by Caspian. The rear sight was positioned rather oddly forward, and the pistol was made of stainless steel, had a reputation for reliable operation, and was expensive. Sophisticated shooters, magazine gun writers, and action-movie producers loved it. Jeff Cooper even had some good things to say about it.

The .45 ACP Detonics CombatMaster was clearly a winner, and the company seemed to be doing well. But by the early '80s, Detonics seemed more interested in talking about new products it had planned for the future, an odd assortment that included double-action 9mm pistols of the type then fashionable and a break-top revolver in the manner of the S&W Schofield. They had also come up with a proprietary .45 auto cartridge (the .451 Detonics Magnum) because that's what you have to do in order to sell guns in countries where civilian ownership of .45 ACP pistols is prohibited. But rather than chamber the oddball cartridge for export only, Detonics tried to promote it in this country as a new, improved .45 ACP. I guess we've all heard that one before. In 1983, a transparently promotional story written by Al Pickles for *American Handgunner* magazine (these were the days when the firearms press was still in the melodramatic throes of its self-created "wondernine" fever) went way over the top in praising the company's blue-sky, nonproduction, non-1911 products. Detonics went out of business shortly thereafter.

The company assets and name were sold to an investor group in Seattle, and Detonics was put on the back shelf to mold, one more victim of the abuse that is so often inflicted on naive entrepreneurial companies by passionless investor types and their bean-counter advisors.

Sometime in '87 or '88, one of the bean counters proclaimed that an attempt should be made to revive Detonics, and the investors made the shockingly good decision to hire Robbie Barrkman to do it for them. Barrkman, of course, is known throughout the firearms community as the founder and president of The Robar Companies, a solid and knowledgeable gun person, an astute businessman, and an honorable gentleman.

Robbie told me,

The original understanding was that Detonics would put out the best .45 on the market. And we did that. We brought the company back. We started again from scratch, with drawings. At first we had all our tooling made by a company in Phoenix, and then we moved it up to Ruger when they put in their foundry. Barrels were all made by Storm Lake Machine. Detonics was the first mass-produced pistol that had all the custom features on it. Everybody's doing that today, but we were way ahead of anybody else. We had the window of opportunity; we were there. The first production run was completely sold out before we ever got it done, and we were back-ordered. If we had done all the

After Robbie Barrkman left Detonics in 1970, he devoted his full time and energy to The Robar Companies. What a good move for all of us. Photo by the author.

things we were supposed to do, Detonics would probably be a very big player in the marketplace today.

But right in the middle of the second production run we ran into political problems. The main money guy decided that he was more interested in something else and he just didn't want to be bothered with it anymore. The investors wanted to go in a different direction, and I was not prepared to put my name on that. They didn't want to do what you're supposed to do to keep up the quality of the product. They wanted to make it cheaper.

I didn't want the company to come to an end, but I wasn't prepared to go on with it if we were not going to do what we were committed to do, which was to put out the best .45 on the market. That was our edge. Anybody can make a .45. I've heard they've been making them since 1911. Detonics had its moment, but instead of seizing it and going with it, these guys started playing their stupid little political games, and it cost them the company.

When Barrkman walked out and closed the doors in 1990, Detonics came to a screeching halt and just lay there for years. The investors didn't try to get anybody else to pick up the ball and run with it. They eventually sold it off again. Which makes Detonics one of those companies that came and went and came and went and is reportedly coming again.

Another newly formed Detonics company, this time located in Atlanta, was present at the SHOT Show 2004. Syd Woodcock, a founder of the original Detonics back in 1976, was there. Woodcock is known as a talented designer, a tinkerer, a nice guy, but not a businessman. The president of the new company is Jerry Ahern, a gun writer and novelist who armed his main fictional hero with a pair of Detonics CombatMasters. The newly tooled prototype Detonics pistols on display included the CombatMaster along with a series of conventionally designed "target" 1911s.

All of the Detonics people present at the SHOT Show were naturally enthusiastic, but they have been rather scarce since. A machine answers their phone, and they don't return e-mail messages. Not a good sign. Let's hope Detonics makes it one more time, but let's not hold our breath. By the time you read this, it may have gone and come and gone again.

In the meantime, Barrkman has gone on to put out his own "best .45 on the market," custom 1911s built to customers' specifications primarily on Springfield and Caspian frames of steel and titanium, with no compromises. The Robar Companies is today a highly successful and multifaceted firm known for its innovative custom gun work and high-tech metal finishes, and Robbie Barrkman has never lost his lifelong affection for the 1911.

"The 1911 is still the basic gun," Barrkman says. "Everybody is building one, and they're selling all the time. Think about it. They're still the mainstay. At this late stage, somebody comes out with a new 1911 and they sell the hell out of it. It's great. The pistol will never die."

## BLINDED BY SUCCESS

Corporations these days do not operate from principles. They do not say, we believe in this kind of gun, and this is the kind of gun we build, and we will not compromise it. Design is too often driven by the marketing department, usually a group of youngsters, too young to have any depth, who have but a mechanical knowledge of the product and could be selling toothpaste just as well. These overtrained, undereducated young executives have no respect for the buyers of their products and care only about coming up with some "improvement" their soulless research tells them will appeal to a sufficiently large number of consumers, anonymous marketing digits who were once called customers. These one-dimensional marketing types have been taught by their couldn't-make-it-in-the-real-world professors to pressure designers to come up with some feature that sets the product apart from the competition, without regard for whether the feature is worthy or not.

Kimber is no exception to this rule. It is no better, though most of the guns it makes are better than a lot of others. It is no worse, though it would be nice to think that a gun maker as good as Kimber would not take seriously the parroted advice from some nitwit with a master's degree in marketing. I use Kimber as an example in this case only because a recent Kimber product provides such a good illustration of the unfortunate fact that even the best of companies will sometimes throw a half-baked product out into the marketplace in the hope that somebody will bite.

The Kimber Ultra RCP II is one of the world's smallest and lightest 1911-pattern .45s, but it handles as well as any man-size gun should. Impeccable craftsmanship, crisp controls, reliable operation. Feels and shoots like something that's ready to save your life, which is important because that's what it's supposed to do. It's almost perfect.

The only real problem with the Ultra RCP II (besides the silly name) is that it represents a gross misinterpretation of important fundamental data—gross enough to be almost unbelievable. If CIA analysts were so harebrained, the United States and its allies would be gearing up for a preemptive nuclear attack on Patagonia because they don't have nearly enough toilets down there and all the ones they do have flush in the wrong direction. Whoever first pointed out that most gunfights take place at extremely close range

undoubtedly expected that observation to lead instructors to focus more training on short-range gun-handling skills, not cause manufacturers to chop the sights off their pistols.

Kimber's efforts were undoubtedly well intentioned. Gun makers have been whittling away on the Colt Government Model 1911 for 50 years, including Colt, first with its Commander and then with its Officer's ACP. Armand Swenson showed everybody how it could be done. Devel and Detonics left their small footprints in a rather large way. Everybody makes a three-inch 1911 these days, and some are every bit as good, as reliable, as shootable as the original five-inch. Some are even better. You can put Kimber in that column, and their latest ultracompact models are the best yet. Except for this one odd thing about this one little gun.

The first thing you notice when you hold the RCP (Refined Carry Pistol) in a firing grip is that it feels like a real gun, not a handful of sharp metal objects. It might as well be a full-size .45, only it's a lot handier, quicker, and far more concealable. Edges are rounded and blended in a carry melt. The mainspring housing is smooth, and the match-grade trigger feels solid. It seems that hardware has finally caught up with the shall-issue concealed-carry laws that have spread throughout the nation in all but the darkest, bluest pockets of reactionary socialism.

The reassuring sense of control continues as you pump 7+1 rounds of 230-grain hollowpoints through the little gun's three-inch barrel, instantly recharge, and keep on going. This is a 26-ounce aluminum-frame 1911 you can shoot all day long. Ergonomics is the short way to describe the applied science of human factors engineering that makes this gun a whole lot friendlier than the academics who talk like that. Crucial controls are properly shaped and precisely tuned. The frame heel is rounded, hammer and thumb safety are tactically bobbed, and the abbreviated beavertail grip safety is just enough to give you a nice, high grip without reminding you of the tail fins on your uncle's '59 Cadillac.

The trigger is of the proverbial glass-rod-breaking type. Unlike the Series 80 system, the Kimber trigger is unencumbered by the need to

The author loved the little Kimber RCP II except for one blinding oversight in the design. Photo by Morgan W. Boatman.

You can see, or rather not see, the problem you're faced with if you have no sights on your gun. Photo by Morgan W. Boatman.

operate the firing-pin block. On the new Kimbers, this questionable chore is taken over by the grip safety, perhaps a better way to do a job that doesn't really need to be done in the first place. Whether as a result of that cleaner trigger design or a superb tuning job at the factory, this trigger on this little Kimber is about as good as it gets, and that is very good indeed.

The slim Micarta grip panels are fluted to integrate with the fluted front strap. The entire grip, smaller than usual though it may be, is magically shaped to snuggle up comfortably in the palm of a normal-size hand. Your little finger has room to perform its job without the aid of an additional shelf on the bottom of the magazine. The gun is so well balanced and so smooth in operation, thanks in part to the heavy bushingless bull barrel and the dual-captured recoil spring design, that it soaks up recoil as well as a big steel pistol. The Kimber does not scratch, claw, strike, sting, or bite back. If this is what they pay them to do all day at Kimber's Custom Shop, it's easy to see where all that money goes.

Honestly, the gun is so good it's a shame that it's expected to tuck its gaping 45-caliber muzzle beneath its wing and spend every sunny day quietly in the dark beneath an expensive Italian

suit to be heard from only in the case of a dire emergency. And it's really a shame that your chances of hitting anything with it further away than the statistically sanctioned seven yards are about the same as if you tied a scarf over your eyes and threw a rock. The gun doesn't have any sights.

The idea of a "sighting trench" is not new. I have a charming little double-action-only .25 automatic made by CZ with a gutter machined down the top of the slide just like the Kimber. It was made in the 1940s, the era when Raymond Chandler's femmes fatales were going around dropping guys left and right with one yank of the triggers of the pearl-handled .25 ACP Colts and Brownings they always kept in their sequined purses, typically heart shots at powder-burn range. The criminal class just ain't what it used to be.

Granted that, on average, most encounters calling for the participation of a powerful little gun do take place at near-contact distance, the haunting fact remains that the one you walk into one day may not. The superb handling and shooting characteristics of the RCP that encourage you to reach out and make somebody's day at 50 yards if necessary are wasted if you don't have anything to cover your target with that's any more precise than a chunk of steel slide. Forget your training in the Modern Technique—you can't focus on the front sight if there is no front sight to focus on. Thus, one of the potentially finest 1911s ever to come down the pike is reduced to the primitive state of a pointing weapon, suitable only for extremely close-range work, preferably by seductive female assassins, destined to be truly loved only by those "instinctive" shooters who believe the way to end a gunfight is to hold your pistol out in front of you, close your eyes, and start pulling the trigger.

The thing is, there is no earthly justification for it. You might reason that front and rear sights could snag in your pocket (or your purse) if you carried the gun there, but this is no pocket or purse pistol. It's a 1911 with a hammer, though a minimal one, which is supposed to remain cocked at all times, which means that it has pocket-snagging ability in its DNA and therefore requires a holster anyway. All decent holsters these days have built-in sight channels because all decent holster makers recognize that guns have sights.

Any small defense gun will sooner or later be compared with the old reliable .38 Special J-frame S&W. The little J-frame also has a sighting trench, but it's been cut to provide a square notch at the rear and ramped up to a post in the front, a simple system that has proved itself virtually snag-free in a lot more pockets, purses, and holsters than all the Kimbers ever made and that, in the right hands, is quite capable of making anybody's day at 50 yards or even more.

Noted custom pistolsmith Terry Tussey has built slick little 1911s with sighting trenches, but he's never forgotten to put a usable front sight at the top end of the ditch.

Bottom line, Kimber introduced the Ultra RCP II with quite a bit of fanfare, and it hasn't been heard from since. You have to dig deep in the Kimber Web site to find a mention of it. It's referred to as a Custom Shop 2003 Special Edition, which means We Tried It But It Didn't Work. No kidding.

The reason I'm taking up space to write about a failed product is because I find the underlying motivation that produced it rather offensive. That a company would tool up and make such an inappropriate product seems to me to reflect a lack of understanding about what they're doing, or a willingness to sell such a product to a naive buyer who, if he's lucky, will live to regret it. Full-caliber defense pistols with no sights. Push-feed rifles chambered in dangerous-game cartridges. Hunting clothes with screeching Velcro closures. They must hire pimply-faced designers straight out of college.

It's too bad, really. The Kimber (insert silly name here) was a great little gun with all kinds of highly desirable features. All they had to do was put some damn sights on it so somebody could shoot something with it.

## THE REAL GUNSITE GUNS

A joint venture between Gunsite Academy and Colt's Manufacturing has produced an elegant piece called Colt's Gunsite Pistol. It's a full five-inch Series 70 gun fitted with niceties

Okay, Buz Mills wants to know why none of us are carrying the official Colt's Gunsite Pistol. What should we tell him? Photo by the author.

If you can't see the Commander-size Colt on the colonel's hip, it's because you're not particularly supposed to. Photo by the author.

like a Novak rear sight in combination with a Heinie front sight, a grooved front strap, a Chip McCormick hammer and sear, thin rosewood grips, a flat mainspring housing, a modestly beveled magazine well with Wilson magazines, a carry melt, and all the usual trigger and reliability work.

The gun also sports a few more or less useless features like an extended thumb safety, the grossly extravagant gullwing beavertail grip safety from Smith and Alexander, a short trigger only a midget could love, and unsightly front cocking serrations on the slide for those who never owned a 1911 equipped with the recoil-spring plunger John Browning designed and therefore never learned a proper press-check.

All in all, the Gunsite Colt is a fine and serviceable pistol once you get past the hype and correct the copywriter-inspired attributes you find inappropriate. You can buy one at the Gunsite "pro shop." Or, if you're taking a class there and

your own gun crashes beyond repair, you can rent one. Presumably, the Gunsite staff can buy them at a substantial discount.

The thing is, I've spent quite a lot of time all over Gunsite Ranch during the last couple of years observing classes and gathering material and interviewing people from Colonel Cooper on down for books and magazine articles, and I've never seen a Colt's Gunsite Pistol in anybody's holster. It's quite possible there was one and I missed it. I'm just reporting what I have and have not seen.

It seems to me that the Gunsite instructors' (and Colonel Cooper's) weapon of choice is a Commander-length 1911, Colt Series 70 or Springfield, undoubtedly with the necessary internal trigger and reliability work done to perfection, but with no visible modifications other than the fact that they are universally equipped with really good sights.

In fact, the most promising equipment innovation to come out of Gunsite in quite a few years is sights. Between Gunsite and Wayne Novak and XS Sights (formerly Ashley Express), they've come up with a big bead front sight mated to a special-cut rear notch that, forgive me, is a sight for sore eyes. They're still working on perfecting it, and I guarantee you will never see it on a factory-made gun because copywriters, being mostly 19-year-old druggies with far better eyesight than mental capacity, will not be able to figure out what the big deal is.

Nobody needs one more custom-looking pistol with multiple extensions and a beavertail grip safety like a '57 Chevy after a bad accident. But some of us would really appreciate a Gunsite Pistol for the Blind.

Max Joseph
Tactical Firearms Training Team
Huntington Beach, CA
www.tftt.com

Wayne Novak
Novak's Inc.
Parkersburg, WV
www.novaksights.com

# Tuning, Personalizing, Customizing, and Gunsmithing

11

**W**riting about custom combat handguns in the '80s, George Nonte said, "The most common mistake is not too little customizing, but too much. Customizing should have a purpose and not be done just for its own sake."

Patrick Sweeney reports that Jeff Cooper once told him that all the 1911 needs are "sights you can see, a trigger you can manage, and utter reliability."

I once heard Louis Awerbuck give this advice to a student who was asking about all manner of custom features: "Don't put shit on your gun."

Nonte, Cooper, and Awerbuck are right, and the finest 1911s show signs of restraint on the part of their owners. But, given a pistol that is easily disassembled into a table full of parts, each of which can be replaced by another of slightly different shape, feel, and finish, not to mention some additional parts that can be fit onto a slightly modified frame, the temptation is just too great for many people to resist.

It is rather universally agreed that the only things you really need to do to most 1911s is a little tuning for reliability with different bullet shapes: deburr and polish the slide, frame, barrel, and magazine surfaces that come in contact with the cartridge; polish the breechface; polish and bevel the extractor; chamfer or bevel the perimeter of the feed ramp and chamber mouth; and lower the ejection port. The reliability points are the magazine, the breechface, the feed ramp, the chamber throat, and the extractor, all of which need to be checked for smoothness, proper angles, and fit. These days, many of the factories do some if not all of these things for you, so you may only need to make sure they did them right.

This Colt National Match is about 60 years old, predating the "Gold Cup" models. Many things (including Colts) were better in those days when real human beings actually worked on them with their hands. As good as it was to begin with, the gun has still had a lot of custom work done to it. The beavertail grip safety was once an expensive custom part. The idea is that it provides a higher grip on the gun for better control. Beavertails are now almost universally standard on all factory 1911s. Besides the beavertail, personalizations made by the author include a hard-chrome finish, lightweight trigger, tactical thumb safety, full-length guide rod, wedge-shaped mainspring housing, magazine well funnel, pads on all the magazines, and, of course, personalized grips. This gun, with its factory match-grade barrel and hand-honed internal parts, has always been extremely accurate with none of the associated reliability problems commonly found on customized 1911s that have simply been tightened down to achieve smaller groups. Photo by Morgan W. Boatman.

But you're not going to stop there, are you? There is no harm in personalizing your pistol, so long as what you do has no potentially negative effect on its function. And if you're the kind of guy who, once he starts trimming a sprawling bush, can't bring himself to put away the clippers until he's created a French poodle or a symmetrical stump, you'll find plenty of entertainment value in further customizing your 1911.

The parts you can easily replace with new and different ones include springs, pins, grips and grip screws, the slide stop, magazine release, thumb safety, drop-in barrels, and some triggers, guide rods, barrel bushings, hammers, grip safeties, mainspring housings/backstraps, and magazine funnels.

More involved operations, which you may or may not be able to do yourself and which most shooters choose to leave to the expert hands of a good 1911 gunsmith with his specialized tools are trigger and action work, fine-tuning of extractors and ejectors, match barrels that require precision fitting, beavertail grip safeties that require some modification to the frame, sight installation, scope base mounting, and some more involved guide rod/barrel bushing systems, magazine funnels, and ambidextrous thumb safeties.

Specialized procedures that you are well advised to trust to the hands of a professional include milling, cutting, reshaping, texturing, checkering, serrations, and refinishing of the steel, precision slide-to-frame fitting, threading the muzzle, designing and building compensators, and any rechambering you might wish to have done.

If you're building a racegun, let your imagination run wild. If you're building the personal gun you've always wanted, go ahead and get everything you've always thought you wanted. If you're building a carry gun, my best advice to you is to make sure it's absolutely reliable and then leave it the hell alone.

The 1911 lends itself to a level of customization that is impossible with any other gun. Photo by Morgan W. Boatman.

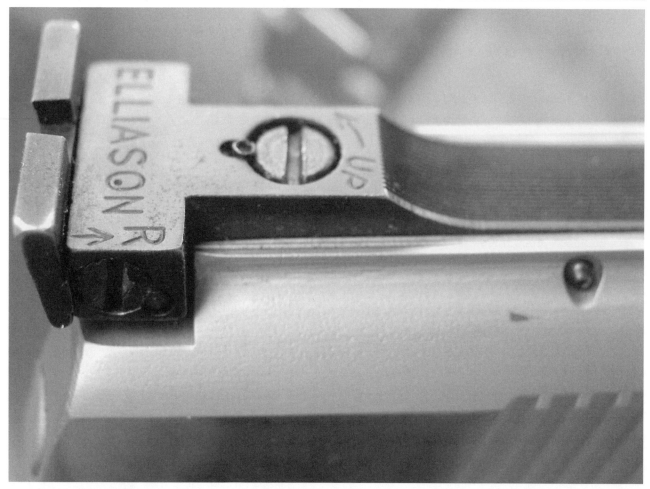

The Colt Elliason rear sight, which has been furnished on Colt's target model 1911s since time immemorial, has a weak retaining pin (far right), which can easily be replaced by a stronger one, as has been done here. If you don't replace the weak pin, the rear sight may launch itself into space under heavy recoil. Once you fix the pin, these sights are excellent for all uses. Photo by Morgan W. Boatman.

Some of the well-known parts makers also build entire guns using only their own parts. So you can buy a Les Baer gun or a Bill Wilson gun. Or you can build up your own gun using anybody's parts you like—install an Ed Brown beavertail grip safety on your Colt, put a McCormick hammer and sear in your Springfield, or turn a Caspian frame over to your favorite gunsmith to use as the basis of a full-on custom. The possibilities are, indeed, endless.

Look over all the bells and whistles. Each will be a useless gimmick, a sexy feature, or a practical benefit, depending on your point of view. Try to control yourself.

Les Baer makes the production version of the Thunder Ranch pistol (Robar makes the full-custom version) as well as his own complete line of semicustom 1911s, plus component parts including the frame.

Baer Custom
Hillsdale, IL
www.lesbaer.com

The easiest way to make your 1911 shoot more accurately is to install a better barrel. Irv Stone of Bar-Sto has been making excellent 1911 replacement barrels for a long time. He'll fit a match-grade barrel to your gun, or he'll send you a "drop-in" barrel that, despite its name, you should still have fitted by a good gunsmith.

Bar-Sto Precision
Twentynine Palms, CA
www.barsto.com

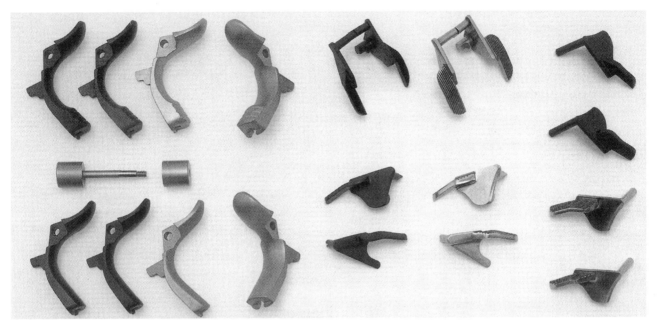

Ed Brown has one of the largest selections of custom 1911 parts you'll ever see. Photo courtesy of Ed Brown Products.

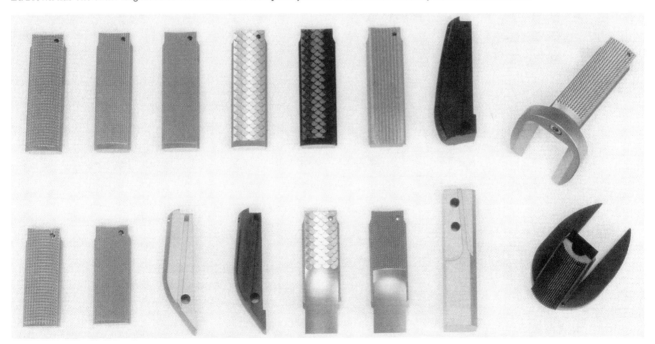

Brown parts are among the most preferred by custom 1911 pistolsmiths. Photo courtesy of Ed Brown Products.

Bob Londrigan of Brazos Custom specializes in complete competition guns built on STI frames as well as a variety of custom gunsmithing products and services.

Brazos Custom Gunworks
Morgan, TX
www.brazoscustom.com

Ed Brown is one of the big custom builders of 1911s and makes a wealth of quality parts for those who would rather build their own.

Ed Brown Products
Perry, MO
www.edbrown.com

Brownells is probably the largest supplier of gun parts in the world. You can almost certainly find whatever you may be looking for in the pages of the catalog. You definitely will find a lot of things you didn't even know you were looking for. Brownells carries the product lines of many manufacturers, and you can build your own custom 1911 just from the parts available in the catalog.

Brownells Inc.
Montezuma, IA
www.brownells.com

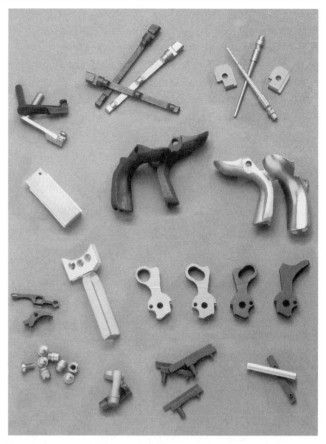

In addition to steel, titanium, and Damascus frames, Caspian makes a variety of other precision parts for your 1911. Photo courtesy of Caspian Arms.

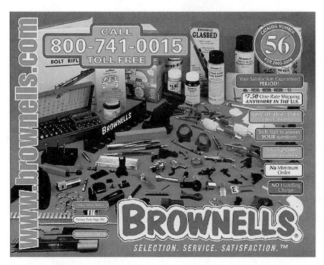

Armed with a Brownells catalog, you can build any kind of 1911 that strikes your fancy. Photo courtesy of Brownells.

Caspian is perhaps best known for its high-quality 1911 frames and slides, forged or cast, in steel, titanium, and even Damascus. Caspian frames are widely used by high-end custom builders to turn out some of the best 1911s you'll ever see.

Caspian Arms
Hardwick, VT
www.caspianarmsltd.8m.com

Chip McCormick makes a variety of precision parts, including one of the most reliable 1911 magazines you can get.

Chip McCormick Corp.
Manchaca, TX
www.chipmccormickcorp.com

Cylinder & Slide owner Bill Laughridge is a 1911 gunsmith who knows what is what. He toured the major IPSC matches in a trailer for years, repairing and rebuilding high-strung raceguns on the spot. He offers a range of custom 1911 parts, does extensive custom work, and is especially known for his immaculate triggers.

Cylinder & Slide
Fremont, NE
www.cylinder-slide.com

Richard Heinie has been building custom 1911 pistols and practical precision sights for them since the '70s. Along with Novak, Heinie sights are among the most respected by serious 1911 shooters.

Heinie Specialty Products
Quincy, IL
www.heinie.com

One of the first things most 1911 owners do is change out the grips, either to achieve a more solid mating between hand and gun or just for beauty's sake. Hogue is one of the oldest grip makers and also represents other lines, both hard rubber and exotic wood.

Hogue Inc.
Paso Robles, CA
www.getgrip.com

Bill Jarvis makes custom 1911 barrels known for their quality. He might also build you a complete custom gun if you ask him just right.

Jarvis Inc.
Hamilton, MT
www.jarvis-custom.com

King's Gun Works has been around since 1949 and offers a variety of factory and custom replacements for virtually every internal and external part in your 1911.

King's Gun Works
Glendale, CA
www.kingsgunworks.com

You'll find Wayne Novak's beautifully designed sights on a lot of factory and custom pistols these days. Wayne offers other products as well, and still builds custom 1911s for people who deserve them.

Novak's Inc.
Parkersburg, WV
www.novaksights.com

Robbie Barrkman of The Robar Companies will build you a custom 1911 from the ground up (Robar makes the full-custom version of the Thunder Ranch pistol) or offer some major custom improvements for the gun you thought was already almost good enough. Robar proprietary finishes, NP3 and Roguard, are famous for their good looks and durability.

The Robar Companies
Phoenix, AZ
www.robarguns.com

Smith & Alexander makes some of the most popular 1911 parts and accessories around, including their widely used magazine guide.

Smith & Alexander
Garland, TX
www.smithandalexander.com

Founded by Virgil Tripp in the '80s, STI is best known for its highly developed competition 1911s. STI frames are also widely used as the heart of custom guns built for competition as well as for more practical uses.

STI
Georgetown, TX
www.stiguns.com

Apparent miracles can sometimes be accomplished by the simple replacement of springs in your 1911. Wolff springs are considered the best.

Wolff Gunsprings
Newton Square, PA
www.gunsprings.com

# The Big
# Three 1911
# Factories

# 12

he 1911 world is dominated by three major manufacturers: Colt, Kimber, and Springfield Armory, not necessarily in that order.

**Colt**, of course, started it all. John Browning was working for Colt when he designed the 1911. Colt was the only manufacturer of 1911s until a world war demanded more guns than the company could supply. It would be many years after both world wars had been concluded, however, before Colt saw any serious competition from other 1911 manufacturers.

Modifications made by Colt to the original Browning design over the years have been slight, few, and far between. Under pressure from the U.S. Army, it fiddled the 1911 into the 1911A1 previously discussed. Under pressure from civilians and custom gunsmiths, it eventually produced the gun in smaller Commander and Officer's Model sizes. Under pressure from antigun politicians, it screwed up the trigger by attaching a firing-pin block contraption to it, which it called the Series 80.

Today, under pressure from a generation of more sophisticated shooters, Colt is again producing Series 70 guns with clean triggers (as Winchester is again producing Mauser-type controlled-round-feed bolt actions, which it dropped in 1964 in a pathetic attempt to cheapen its rifles). Colt is even offering a replica of the original World War I–era 1911, one of its biggest selling models. It's clear that today's more knowledgeable shooters are willing to pay for the obliteration of all the "improvements" perpetrated on them by gun company bean counters. As a result, some previously excellent firearms, the Series 70 Colt 1911 among them, are being returned to their original sound design.

There is still a certain mystique attached to Colt, despite the fact that, like so many of the old-line American gun companies, it is seldom responsive to its market of users and has often been plagued by financial, management, labor union, and quality control problems over the years. You may have an excellent or shoddily built Colt, just as you may have an excellent or shoddily built Winchester. Every time Colt turns out a bad batch of guns, a feeding frenzy begins and a half dozen new companies sprout up holding new 1911s in their hot little hands. Gun makers tend to have an easier time of it the farther away they get from the antigun hotbeds of the country. I wouldn't try to build a fine firearms manufacturing operation in Boston or Chicago or San Francisco if I were you.

Personally, I've always had good luck with Colts. I've never carried a 1911 with any other company's name on it, and I think I would feel funny about it if I did. Jeff Cooper carries a Colt. And so do a lot of other shooters whose names you would not recognize but whose exploits you might.

**Springfield Armory** is a private company that took its name from the old government arsenal. It was the first to see a large hole in a burgeoning market and moved decisively to fill it. In the beginning, Springfield bought its way into the marketplace by making Colt clones at more reasonable prices, not a difficult thing to do. Today, the company maintains its strong position with highly respected guns that are widely recognized for their out-of-the-box shootability and reliable operation. Besides that, Springfield frames have always been among the most popular foundations for full-custom carry and

competition 1911s. An untold number of Springfields are out there in appreciative hands, doing their jobs in every area for which a 1911 is appropriate, which is just about every area one could possibly imagine, including filling the holsters of specially trained FBI agents.

**Kimber** came roaring out of the West with little warning. A company that had made its mark manufacturing high-quality .22 rimfire rifles was suddenly in the 1911 business in a big way, totally unexpectedly and almost overnight it seems. The original company was turned inside out, naturally, and went through reorganizations, false starts, divorce and reconciliation, somersaults and

Even Kimber pistols designed for target shooting are reliable. And those designed for carry are accurate. Photo courtesy of Kimber.

Kimber made a name for itself in the beginning by including the most desirable custom features in a factory gun. Now everybody's doing it. Photo courtesy of Kimber.

The company that used to make nothing but neat little .22 rifles now makes great little .45 autos as well. Photo courtesy of Kimber.

cartwheels, and who knows what political machinations, as nobody I've ever talked to at Kimber will tell the whole truth, or even knows the whole truth, about those transitional days. It doesn't really matter, because the important fact is that Kimber is today one of the strongest forces in the 1911 market, probably the largest in terms of sales, a position earned by offering a quality product emphasizing reliability, accuracy, and standard configurations that include most of the custom features that were traditionally aftermarket and gunsmith items on most other factory guns.

Kimber has marketed aggressively to law enforcement and special military units, showing a willingness to design guns specifically to meet sometimes rather specialized needs. As a result, you'll find quite a few high-speed operators using Kimbers, including LAPD SWAT.

Kimber's latest "improvement" of the 1911 is attaching the firing-pin block to the operation of the grip safety instead of to the trigger as on the Series 80 Colt. Kimber's idea, implemented in all of its Series II pistols, is not a new one. The gadget was called the Swartz safety back in 1937 when William Swartz invented it and Colt tried it out in a few models. It worked fine, but Colt, rightfully, decided it wasn't needed. Forty-three years later, when pressure from the gun banners for useless safety devices reached a peak, Colt decided to reinvent the firing-pin block. Some Colt intern had the bright idea of making the shooter's sensitive trigger finger do all the additional work of operating the unnecessary device instead of letting the fat web of the hand take care of it as in the Swartz design. Oh well, I kind of like the idea of attaching one useless device (the firing-pin block) to another useless device (the grip safety). A gunsmith can undoubtedly wipe them both out with one shot. Kimber has also joined the latest trend of installing external extractors on some of its guns, and we'll have to see how that works out in the long run, since there seems to be equally meaningless arguments on both sides of the issue.

Based on national sales figures and an informal survey I conducted with all of my gun-savvy friends, Kimber is the favored 1911 these days for out-of-the-box reliability and accuracy. Instructor Max Joseph, who is no fan of fancified .45s, tells me, "We're seeing a lot of Kimbers on the line these days. They are reliable and good to go right out of the box. The next gun I buy is going to be a Kimber." From Max Joseph, that is high praise indeed.

The Big Three are not alone. A rash of

Para-Ordnance S14-45 Limited has all the trendy features you can imagine. Photo courtesy of Para-Ordnance.

competitors, established and growing noncustom manufacturers, and importers whose 1911s range from ordinary to extremely good is forever hot on their heels.

**Para-Ordnance** is a Canadian company whose claim to fame is adapting for the 1911 the staggered magazine concept developed by Belgian Dieudonne Saive for the Browning High Power or P-35. By necessity, Para-Ordnance pistols have a wider grip frame than other 1911s, and the resulting higher-capacity magazines—up to 14+1 rounds in a .45—have made them popular with IPSC competitors. High-capacity magazines for the Para-Ordnance have never been a problem to obtain, so the guns are also carried by people who don't mind a fat 1911. Whether or not a wide-body .45 fits your hand is a function of the size of your hand.

Nevertheless, feeling a little cramped in the high-capacity area, the company has lately been promoting its double-action-only models, advertising them as *safer* than cocked-and-locked single-actions, which is about the dumbest thing a 1911 manufacturer could do. They've also been

The Para Warthog is one of the smallest .45 packages you can get. Photo courtesy of Para-Ordnance.

promoting a larger, redesigned internal extractor. Both of these "improvements" show every sign of being solutions to nonexistent problems. However, double-action-only pistols have strong appeal for the cocked-and-locked shy (the untrained shooter, in other words), and if a bigger extractor in fact translates directly into better extraction, that will be a good thing. Only time will tell. Don't hold your breath. It is difficult to know whether heavily promoted new and improved features on guns are the work of experienced firearms engineers or some English-trained creative director at the ad agency.

**Auto Ordnance** still makes Thompsons, as it always has. Now that it's owned by Kahr Arms, it makes higher-quality 1911s as well.

**Olympic Arms** owns Safari Arms, which made a name for itself manufacturing stainless steel 1911s with distinctive finger grooves integral with the front strap. You either like 'em or not. Jeff Cooper owns one.

**Dan Wesson**, of large-frame revolver fame, makes full-size 1911s with external extractors, match-grade barrels, and two-piece, full-length guide rods. I think I would be quicker to buy a 1911 from this Mr. Wesson's company than the one founded by his great-grandfather and Mr. Smith.

Colt Manufacturing Co.
Hartford, CT
www.colt.com

Springfield Armory
Geneseo, IL
www.springfield-armory.com

Kimber of America
Yonkers, NY
www.kimberamerica.com

Para-Ordnance
Scarborough, Ontario, CAN
www.paraord.com

Kahr Arms (Auto Ordnance)
Blauvelt, NY
www.kahr.com (www.tommygun.com)

Olympic Arms
Olympia, WA
www.olyarms.com

Dan Wesson Firearms
Norwich, NY
www.danwessonfirearms.com

# The Big Three Custom Builders

13

**C**ustom pistolsmiths have devoted more love and creativity to the 1911 than Colt, Kimber, and Springfield Armory combined, though the big manufacturers have never hesitated to steal a good custom maker's idea when they could figure out how to produce it in a cheaper, mass-produced kind of way. To be fair, Kimber was smart enough to hire custom gunsmith John Yanek to design its first 1911. Springfield Armory hired custom gunsmith Les Baer to open its Custom Shop. And, of course, Colt hired John Browning in the first place.

Custom gunsmiths have always been the prime movers behind the slow but sure evolution of the gun. Frank Pachmayr, Jim Clark, and Les Baer figured out how to make the 1911 more accurate. Jim Hoag and Ed Brown are responsible for development of the currently ubiquitous beavertail grip safety. Bill Wilson perfected the sometimes temperamental 1911 magazine. Armand Swenson invented the ambidextrous thumb safety and, together with Frank Behlert, Charley Kelsey, and Larry Seecamp, demonstrated with elegance just how small and compact the Government Model could get.

Today, there's a Big Three in custom builders, just as there's a Big Three in factory guns. In both cases, the Big Three represent only the tip of the iceberg.

Bill Wilson, Les Baer, and Ed Brown got where they are by building blindingly beautiful guns with match-grade accuracy and commensurate price tags. The finish, workmanship, fine touches, and attention to detail you'll find on any gun from Wilson Combat, Les Baer Custom, and Ed Brown Products are irreproachable. A lot of shooters who can afford them carry them in alligator-hide holsters and hate like hell that they have to conceal them.

Wilson, Baer, and Brown are all former competition

105

pistol shooters and, to be perfectly honest, the only problem I have with them is that they are oriented to a level of accuracy—I've heard it aptly described as "anal accuracy"—that is irrelevant in a combat gun. This is partially achieved by building a very tightly fitted weapon at the potential cost of functional reliability—a cost I don't think any shooter other than a Sunday afternoon paper-puncher should ever pay.

Max Joseph recently told me, "The last few years I have seen more malfunctions in 1911s than ever before. It's because of gunsmiths—amateurs and even good ones—tightening the action up too much trying to get 2-inch, 50-yard groups." Anal accuracy.

Both Max Joseph and Louis Awerbuck have told me that they like their .45s to rattle when they shake them. Wilson and Baer and Brown .45s don't rattle. Your custom gun may run faultlessly when it gets full of dust and grit and unburned powder particles and sweat and blood and bug juice. Or it may not. It may be 99 percent reliable 99 percent of the time, which you may or may not find acceptable. As the old saying goes, "You pays your money and you takes your chances." With these guys, you definitely pays your money. And if you do have reliability or any other problems with one of their custom guns, I'm sure they will fix it to the best of their abilities in short order—short of making it rattle.

Frankly, the Big Three custom builders have gotten so big they have standardized most of their models, and most of the guns they sell these days are more accurately described as semicustoms. They are still capable of building you a true custom gun if you can afford it, but they are by no means the only custom builders in the market.

Garey O. Hindman of Ace Custom .45s specializes in converting 1911-pattern pistols to the .45 Super cartridge. He also offers finished custom guns and a complete gunsmithing service. The .45 Super, a concept created by gun writer Dean Grennell, is built on brass with thicker walls and a heavier web area to withstand the higher pressures of increased velocity. Guns so chambered will also fire .45 ACP rounds.

Ace Custom 45s
Cleveland, TX
www.acecustom45s.com

Les Baer was making a name for himself building custom 1911s when Springfield Armory hired him to start its highly respected Custom Shop. Baer's talent bought Springfield a lot of credibility, and Baer learned a lot about larger-scale manufacturing from the big company too. Back on his own, Baer today makes a wide variety of custom guns and parts, and he does not hesitate to guarantee the precision accuracy of his pistols.

Baer Custom
Hillsdale, IL
www.lesbaer.com

Bob Londrigan of Brazos Custom Gunworks builds competition guns that look like they came right off the set of the next Star Wars movie. But he can also turn his talents to more practical matters, like delivering you a refined tool to save your life.

Brazos Custom Gunworks
Morgan, TX
www.brazoscustom.com

Brazos Custom Gunworks BCG Pro Series Limited built on an STI frame. Brazos is known for its advanced competition guns from Limited to Open, plus a very nice carry gun on a highly modified Springfield Ultra Compact .45. Photo courtesy of BCG.

Claudio Salassa built 1911s in South Africa when the United States and the rest of the world refused to send guns or parts or anything else to that country. When he moved from South Africa to Houston he started building 1911s for a company previously known for its fine shotguns. The Briley Pistol Division offers Salassa custom guns built to order and a select line of parts, including Salassa's esteemed spherical-bushing match barrels.

Briley Pistol Division/Claudio Salassa
Houston, TX
www.briley.com

Ed Brown 1911s are among the most highly regarded, and his diverse line of aftermarket parts

Ed Brown Executive Carry model has the comfortable-to-shoot bobbed backstrap and sports many of the builder's highly regarded custom parts. Photo courtesy of Ed Brown.

Ed Brown Kobra models feature Ed's unique engraved steel snakeskin pattern. Photo courtesy of Ed Brown.

and accessories are certainly among the most widely used by custom gunsmiths throughout the country. Brown, who started working on 1911s when he was a teenager and is a former world-class IPSC shooter, attributes his success not to his shooting skills but to engineering excellence, precision manufacturing, hand craftsmanship, performance, and a wide variety of options made possible by flexible manufacturing technology. Brown claims, with some justification, that his family-run company offers more selection and customization than you can get anywhere else.

Ed Brown Products
Perry, MO
www.edbrown.com

The firm of Jim Clark Sr. and Jim Clark Jr. is one of the oldest gunsmithing services around. The Clark name is highly respected in the firearms community, and the company manufactures a good variety of very high-quality 1911 parts, not to mention the occasional custom gun.

Clark Custom Guns
Princeton, LA
www.clarkcustomguns.com

Dave Dawson builds high-capacity IPSC raceguns on the one hand and tactical guns for special forces military on the other. He particularly likes to work with STI frames and offers a line of parts and accessories as well.

Dawson Precision
Leander, TX
www.competitionshooters.com

Dick Heinie has been a fixture in the 1911 world practically forever, and he has never done anything that hasn't been very interesting and of very high quality. Best known for his sights and his custom gunsmithing, Heinie has also been known to build an incredible custom pistol or two.

Heinie Specialty Products Inc.
Quincy, IL
www.heinie.com

Paul Liebenberg is another South African custom gunsmith who left his country. He went to work for Pachmayr Gun Works, was director of S&W's Performance Center, and now builds his own custom guns primarily on Caspian frames and slides. The spirit of Frank Pachmayr is alive and well.

Paul Liebenberg/Pistol Dynamics
Palm Bay, FL

Wayne Novak is known for his sleek, carry-oriented sight systems, but the man has been building high-end custom 1911s since the beginning of time, even working for Armand Swenson back in the early days. Wayne is still at it, and his custom guns are better than ever.

Novak's Inc.
Parkersburg, WV
www.novaksights.com

This is a full-house Novak Kimber. Photo courtesy of Wayne Novak.

Wayne Novak combined a Colt frame with a Caspian Damascus slide, added a Kart barrel, Pete Simple checkering, and Craig Spegel grips, along with his own custom sights, parts, and expert workmanship to come up with this beauty. Note the Novak "Practical Grip Screws," which turn with both an Allen wrench and standard screwdriver. Photo courtesy of Wayne Novak.

Novak Colt Custom features Novak Extreme Duty rear sight with gold bead front, Kart ramped barrel with a Novak bushing. Photo courtesy of Wayne Novak.

Founded by John Nowlin Sr., Nowlin Manufacturing specializes in competition guns and precision 1911 barrels for more demanding applications. The company also makes an expanding line of other 1911 parts.

Nowlin Mfg. Co.
Claremore, OK
www.nowlinguns.com

Kase Reeder of Reeder Custom Guns is the son of famous pistol maker Gary Reeder, and they both work in the same spacious shop. While Gary is working on his world-renowned, big-bore revolvers, Kase is turning out fighting-oriented 1911s. Kase grew up peering over his father's workbench with heroes like Armand Swenson, and he has both the talent and the ambition to make a name for himself. As far as a lot of savvy 1911 people are concerned, he already has. He's still young; take advantage of him.

Reeder Custom Guns
Flagstaff, AZ
www.reedercustomguns.com

Robbie Barrkman of Robar will build his full-custom Thunder Ranch, Deluxe, or Combat Master pistol on the 1911 frame of your choice. Robbie knows the difference between gewgaws and important enhancements on a defensive weapon, and you will find only the latter on the guns he builds, whether pistol, rifle, or shotgun.

The Robar Companies
Phoenix, AZ
www.robarguns.com

Kase Reeder is committed to the idea that form follows function, just like his childhood hero Armand Swenson. Photo courtesy of Reeder Custom Guns.

A Kase Reeder 1911 is something you can admire, go out and pump a few hundred rounds through, and then bring back and admire some more. Photo courtesy of Reeder Custom Guns.

Robar's Thunder Ranch pistol is built to perform any job you might decide to assign it. Photo courtesy of The Robar Companies.

In addition to custom work and parts, STI offers a standard line of 1911s, both single- and double-stack with polymer grip frames. The company's primary target is the competition shooter, but the exotic looks of many STI guns appeal to a larger audience.

STI
Georgetown, TX
www.stiguns.com

Terry Tussey may be best known for building real guns for movie hero Steven Seagal, but when I first met him something like 25 years ago, he was

Terry Tussey believes a carry gun might as well be beautiful, and the Caspian Damascus slide, ivory grips, and other characteristic Tussey touches on this gorgeous little custom piece (too bad it has to be carried concealed) sure ain't ugly. Photo Courtesy of Tussey Custom.

Terry Tussey at work. He works on a gun until he's satisfied. He'll let you know when he's finished. Photo courtesy of Tussey Custom.

A compensated .38 Super that Terry built especially for a special lady. Photo courtesy of Tussey Custom.

building real guns for guys like me. My Tussey/Colt Officer's ACP is still one of my favorites, and it works just as well today as it did a quarter century ago. Terry knows what a defense gun has to be, but he has nothing against making them pretty at the same time. He's been doing a lot of full-custom guns with Caspian stainless·Damascus slides lately, and they're gorgeous to look at as well as very practical, functional pistols. I'm just glad he still builds guns for guys like me.

Tussey Custom
Carson City, NV
www.tusseycustom.com

Dave Van Horn of Van Horn Custom/The Gun Shop has been building full-custom guns of every description for 22 years. One gun at a time. Everything he touches is custom—1911s, big-

game, mountain, and varmint rifles built on every kind of action there is, precision barrels including the super lightweight carbon-fiber kind, and did I mention 1911s? Dave invented the Thompson/Center carbine, a whole bunch of custom calibers from .14 to .50, and a lot more. If you want a true craftsman to build you a 1911, you couldn't do any better than David Van Horn. The guns he's built for me are among the ones I wouldn't trade for anything.

Van Horn Custom/The Gun Shop
Gilbert, AZ
www.mygunroom.com/dvgunshop

Larry Vickers is an active-duty Special Forces operator who builds fewer than a dozen 1911s a year. By hand. His guns are immaculate, and his waiting list is long. You might want to think about getting in line.

Dave Van Horn builds custom 1911s that are meant to be carried. He carries one himself, and he makes sure it works! Photo by the author.

L.A. Vickers Custom
Fayetteville, NC

In the early days of IPSC, Bill Wilson toured with the circuit in the dual roles of serious competitor and unofficial gunsmith to his rivals. For years, this former watchmaker built more IPSC competition guns, including the first raceguns, than anybody else. More concerned with 1911s for self-defense these days, Wilson forges his own frames and slides and produces probably more 1911 parts than anybody else. You'll see complete Wilson pistols in every application, along with any number of Wilson parts on other guns, and you'll find a Wilson magazine in almost every serious 1911 you look at.

Wilson Combat
Berryville, AR
www.wilsoncombat.com

# The
# Unexpected

 nyone who doubts the timeless nature of John Browning's 1911 design need only look at the unexpected companies who are introducing "new" 1911 pistols for the first time.

**Smith & Wesson**, Colt's traditional adversary, which in the past has taken its antagonism so far as to make the safeties of its semiautos work backward from Colt's and the cylinders of its revolvers turn in the opposite direction, has finally come around. In fact, to S&W's undoubted chagrin, Jeff Cooper calls this new S&W 1911 "the Smith & Wesson Colt."

The slab-sided Smith with "1911" emblazoned on its slide is stainless steel with an external extractor, Novak LoMount sights, Chip McCormick thumb safety and full-length guide rod, Wilson Combat beavertail, Texas Armament trigger, Briley barrel bushing, Hogue grips, Wolff springs, and a grip-safety-operated firing-pin block à la old Colt and new Kimber. In fact, S&W has been supplying forgings to Kimber for its slides and frames for a number of years and produces semifinished frames and other components for Dan Wesson 1911 pistols and others as well. When you've got any number of different companies all building essentially the same pistol, a little incest is inevitable, folks.

Smith & Wesson
Springfield, MA
www.smith-wesson.com

**SIGARMS**, the Swiss firm famous for its engineering, was the first factory, as I recall, to produce a double-action .45 ACP, best described then and now as clunky. The firm's

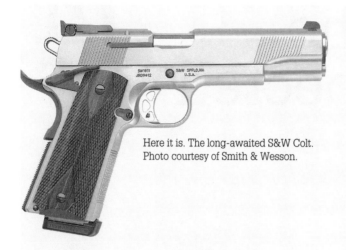

Here it is. The long-awaited S&W Colt. Photo courtesy of Smith & Wesson.

**Heckler & Koch**, the German arms manufacturer that has always prided itself on its ultramodern, forward-looking designs, may be looking over its shoulder. Rumor has it that H&K will build a 1911. If it does, and if there are any real improvements to be made in John Browning's almost perfected design, Heckler & Koch is a likely company to discover and implement them.

Heckler & Koch
Sterling, VA
www.hk-usa.com

new full-size 1911 is anything but. Built in full-size stainless steel with matte or black finish, the SIG refreshingly deletes the guide rod and accompanying forward cocking serrations and adds an integral light rail and external extractor. Novak makes good sights and magazines for the new 1911, it is reputedly quite accurate and reliable, and SIG calls it a GSR for reasons you really don't care about.

SIGARMS
Exeter, NH
www.sigarms.com

**CZ**, Ceská Zbrojovka to you, already makes some of the world's best non-1911 pistols and Mauser-action rifles. Now that the country has rid itself of its Communist overseers (we can only hope the United States will one day do the same) and is once again a free country, the great Czech gun maker is getting serious again. Rumors about new CZ guns have been circulating for some time. One, that there will be a new dangerous-game, magnum-action rifle in the grand, old British caliber .505 Gibbs, the company has confirmed. The other, that there will be a CZ 1911, it denies. We can only hope.

If CZ does, in fact, build a 1911, you can bet it

**Unertl**, whose founder developed Germany's great World War II sniper scope, is now under new U.S. ownership and has expanded beyond optics into the surprising field of 1911 manufacture. The Unertl Ordnance 1911A1 (the MEU-SOC model) has all the state-of-the-art features, including an ambidextrous thumb safety, beavertail grip safety, slide rails, etc. and comes with a Teflon finish in your choice of green, black, gray, or desert camouflage.

Unertl Ordnance Co.
Las Vegas, NV
www.unertloptics.com

Look for a proliferation of S&W 1911 models as the gun (very probably) gains wider acceptance. Photo courtesy of Smith & Wesson.

will be a good one. I own a couple of vintage CZ pistols and a half dozen CZ 550 Magnum big-game rifles, and I'm high on the waiting list for the new .505. I like them. They work. CZ knows what it's doing.

CZ USA
Kansas City, KS
www.cz-usa.com

# The Future of the Fighting Gun

# 15

The 1911 was born at exactly the right time to participate in all of the great battles and wars of the 20th century. John Browning, in addition to his other talents, may have been psychic. There was a time after World War II when Americans believed that the last war of all time had been fought and won decisively and that was the end of it. There was no longer any need for such an implement as the 1911 pistol. We, alone in all the world, had the atomic bomb, why would anybody ever need a primitive old .45 ever again?

This way of thinking preceded our growing awareness of the gigantic monster of Communism that the second war to end all wars had injected with steroids. This was before we recognized that Frank Roosevelt's lethal alliances had already poisoned our own government, that the toxin was spreading throughout vulnerable nations around the world and thriving on our own college campuses as well as in our federal bureaucracies, suburban living rooms, and city streets. This was before the seeds planted by leftist politicians in the days after World War II suddenly burst forth in the worldwide religious war that began on September 11, 2001.

It was at this point that America realized slaying the alien beast was no longer enough—it was too late; we had already been infected; the enemy without had become the enemy within. So America shed its innocence, reached in to retrieve the old .45 from its World War II trunk, dusted it off, loaded it up, and placed it carefully in the drawer of its nightstand.

Through it all, the 1911 never left the holster of the well-trained soldier. But after periods of civilian neglect and minor roles as a collectors' item, object of amusement and games, and joystick for the frustrated modern male, the 1911 found its way into more and more concealed holsters of armed and vigilant American citizens, a place where it has always belonged.

The military 1911 sports all the latest electronic gadgetry, whereas the civilian 1911 shows more subtle signs of evolution, influenced by the official and unofficial warriors who have put it to good use for almost a hundred years and, above all, by the philosophical focus of Col. Jeff Cooper.

As usual, the big gun companies often find themselves following the lead of more adventuresome, imaginative, and entrepreneurial gun builders who do not operate under the burdens of automated production lines, toothpaste-oriented marketing departments, and obstructive little gangs of lawyers.

The timeless design of the 1911 has a special appeal to many of these small custom builders. Some turn out guns that are superior to factory models in every way. Others do not really understand the fighting premise of the 1911 and build guns that are good-looking and quite accurate but ruinously unreliable. If you want a good 1911, you have to find a gunsmith who knows his way around combat pistols, not one who has spent his life building persnickety target guns.

There are two powerful trends in the 1911 world that show every sign of lasting for a very long time. Both are entirely compatible with the spirit of the fighting gun, though the two trends lead off along quite different design paths. One is the trend toward ever more compact, more concealable defense guns. The other is the trend toward recapturing the timeless look and feel of Browning's original, a "retro" movement if you will, that nevertheless produces an entirely practical and satisfying pistol for defense.

In the compact-carry area, there is not a 1911 manufacturer who does not produce one or a dozen models directly for this market. Many custom pistolsmiths specialize in building these powerful little guns. In the retro area, Colt, Springfield Armory, and Auto Ordnance/Kahr are producing World War I and World War II models in

Thanks, Colonel Cooper. Photo by the author.

more or less original configuration and can't keep up with the demand. Dick Heinie and Larry Vickers have recently built custom retro masterpieces.

Shooters will always play games with their guns. Competition will always spark keen interest in objects intended for a far more serious purpose. In the past, games fashioned by people defined the kinds of guns that would be made. In the future, the guns will define the games.

The following message, recently received from a professional operator and instructor, pretty well sums up the attitude of the fighting man toward his fighting gun:

Last weekend, we had a student show up with a Colt Gold Cup, 1911. It lasted for 100 rounds, then stopped feeding, because the recoil spring was so weak. The rear sight also came loose. We pulled it off the line and replaced it with a S&W 1911, which worked just fine for the rest of the weekend. I warn students to stay away from any gun that says "target" or "match," or, for that matter, any gun that the maker boasts is capable of anal accuracy. I believe anal accuracy and reliability are inherently incompatible, and I therefore have no interest in "accurate" guns. I like utility, working guns that are designed and built for serious, not trivial, purposes. The 1911 system gets screwed with so much by gunsmiths and manufacturers alike in an effort to make it hyper-accurate, it is getting an unhappy

reputation. Real 1911s are plenty accurate for any serious purpose.

So much for the gun. But the colonel said that mind-set is everything. A willingness to take the step. So let me leave you with a thought that may be a good thing for you to remember as you slip your *real* 1911 into its holster and go forth into the brave new world: always fire a couple of warning shots into your enemy's chest before you blow his brains out.

# The 1911 as Art

## 16

**S**ailing ships, high-speed airplanes and race-cars, powerful longbows, dueling swords, and firearms are inherently beautiful. Not because a clever designer invented their beauty but because they must look the way they look and be the way they are in order to function in their rigorously defined roles.

Even before the Germans ushered industrial design into the world of art and formalized the concept that form should follow function, the 1911 was appreciated as a thing of beauty. The unadorned lines of Browning's semiautomatic pistol are as graceful as anything in nature. And its flat surfaces present a fine canvas for the nonfunctional but nonetheless handsome art of the steel engraver.

Sheriff Jim Wilson, a practical man, recalls when he was running a gunshop and also working at the Denton County Sheriff's Office, and so had a little extra money to buy handguns for his own use:

> West Texas Wholesale had bought a bunch of factory-engraved Colt 1911s from the Custom Shop and was offering them at plumb reasonable prices. After a good deal of cogitation, I decided to order a blue-steel, D-engraved Government Model. It cost me right at $800. This fancy auto was of the '70-series design that featured the flanged bushing for improved accuracy. It also had one of the best factory triggers that I have ever found on a .45 automatic. A set of carved ivory grips was added to sort of gild the lily, and I had the finest .45 auto that I have ever owned. This engraved 1911 is the gun that generally accompanies me in my duties as a county sheriff. It shoots to point of aim with most brands of 230-grain hollowpoint ammunition and

has never jammed. A good-looking handgun that shoots well too is one of life's little joys. Long ago, I made the decision that I couldn't abide fancy guns that were meant to be hung on the wall. I'll keep on packing this engraved Colt and let my son hang it on the wall, assuming he wants to, after I'm gone.

Bauhaus, baroque, or government issue, plain, fancy, or all beat-up, you only have to look at a 1911 to recognize its intended purpose and to feel confident that it is capable of getting the job done.

The beautiful work depicted in this chapter is courtesy of the following custom gunmakers, engravers, and artists:

Russell and Chick Menard
CAM Enterprises
Mayer, AZ
fiftycalgal@commspeed.net

Kirkpatrick Leather
Laredo, TX
www.kirkpatrickleather.com

Mike Morgan, engraver
Dixon, CA
rockinmqtr@aol.com

Wayne Novak
Novak's Inc.
Parkersburg, WV
www.novaksights.com

Kase Reeder
Reeder Custom Guns
Flagstaff, AZ
www.reedercustomguns.com

Terry Tussey
Tussey Custom
Carson City, NV
www.tusseycustom.com

Factory Springfield Armory 1911A1 .38 Super. Photo by the author.

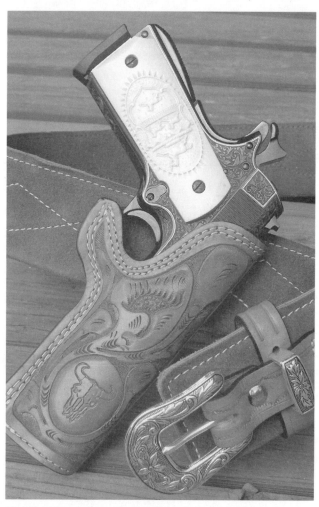

Pre–World War II Colt ornately engraved by Mike Morgan finds a comfortable home in this Holdridge rig hand-tooled by Kirkpatrick Leather. Photo by Morgan W. Boatman.

Factory Springfield Armory 1911A1 .38 Super. Photo by the author.

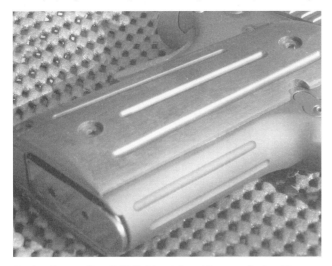

Kimber Custom Shop RCP II .45 with fluted frame and grips. Photo by the author.

Even the most beautiful guns in the world are made to be shot. Photo by Morgan W. Boatman.

Colt National Match manufactured in 1938. Engraving and 14-karat gold inlay by Mike Morgan of Dixon, California. Mike says he spent more than 300 hours on this Colt. Bluing by Brian Rebuck of American Bluing Company in Rodeo, California, a favorite resource used by custom engravers and gunsmiths. This is one of the few Colts equipped with the Swartz Safety, which operates a firing-pin block off the grip safety/hammer. The current Kimber system is a near duplicate of the Swartz system. Photo by Morgan W. Boatman.

Stainless steel Randall Service Model .45. Engraving and gunsmithing by Chick Menard, CAM Enterprises. Photo by the author.

Stainless steel Randall Service Model .45. Engraving and gunsmithing by Chick Menard, grips by Russell Menard, CAM Enterprises. Photo by the author.

This is one of the first custom 1911s Wayne Novak ever built, even before he started making his own famous sights. The gun features French border engraving, a Kart barrel, hand-matted top of slide, and a set of BoMar sights. Photo courtesy of Wayne Novak.

Novak Commemorative to celebrate the one millionth Novak sight sold. This is a full-house custom and Wayne Novak's personal Colt. Photo courtesy of Wayne Novak.

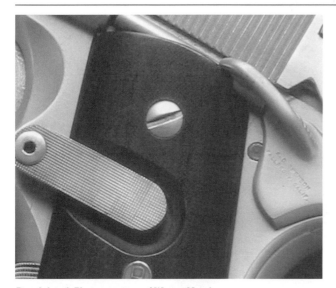

Devel detail. Photo courtesy of Wayne Novak.

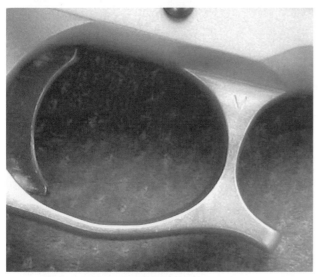

Devel detail. Photo courtesy of Wayne Novak.

Right: Custom Colt Commander .45 with bobbed heel and see-through grip panel. Gunsmithing by Kase Reeder. Photo courtesy of Reeder Custom Guns.

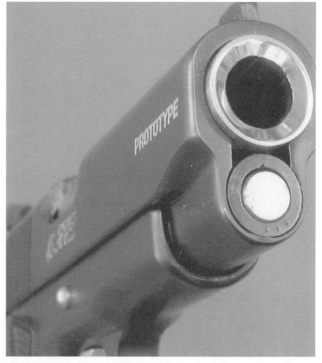

Custom Colt .45 by Kase Reeder. Photo by the author.

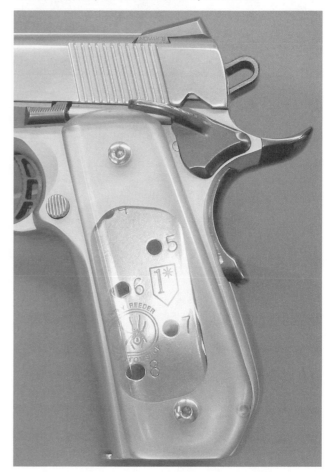

Terry Tussey Colt. Ivory grips are from the Colt factory circa 1938! Photo courtesy of Tussey Custom.

Terry Tussey Colt. Engraving by Mike Morgan. Photos courtesy of Tussey Custom.

# Addendum
# Judging the Judges
## A Dissenting Opinion

The Ninth Circuit Court of Appeals in San Francisco, California, has jurisdiction over 56 million American citizens. Virtually every news organization in the country, from the *New York Times* to the Associated Press, has at one time or another accurately described it as the largest, the most liberal, and the most overturned federal court in the United States. Between 1990 and 1996, the U.S. Supreme Court struck down 73 percent of the Ninth Circuit's rulings. In 1997, the Supreme Court overturned 27 out of 28 of the Ninth Circuit Court's decisions. But even the Supreme Court can't always control the Ninth Circuit. Legal author Ronald Branson, who has studied the Ninth Circuit Court for years, cites cases where the court has ignored and defied Supreme Court decisions it doesn't agree with. A former California assemblyman and author of *The Judicial Accountability Initiative Law*, Branson refers to the Ninth Circuit Court of Appeals as "The Enemy Within."

Packed with Jimmy Carter and Bill Clinton appointees, the Ninth Circuit Court's most notorious judge is Stephen Reinhardt, perhaps best known nationally as the judge who declared the Pledge of Allegiance unconstitutional. Locally, Reinhardt is known as the fifth (so far) husband of the woman who heads the Los Angeles branch of the ACLU, cofounded the rabidly feminist group NARAL (National Abortion and Reproduction Rights Action League), and is a leader of the left-wing-extremist organization People for the American Way, thus begging for a quote from Freud's *General Introduction to Psychoanalysis:* "A fear of weapons is a sign of retarded sexual and emotional maturity."

In December 2002, in hearing the case *Silveira v. Lockyer,* an attempt by concerned citizens to have the California Assault Weapons Ban ruled unconstitutional, a three-judge panel of the Ninth Circuit issued a 69-page magnum opus interpreting the 27 words of the Second Amendment in a way that contradicts a recent federal appellate court decision, the opinion of the attorney general of the United States, and the common sense of every gun owner in America. Judge Stephen Reinhardt decided that the Second Amendment only protects the state's collective right to own firearms and that the Constitution does not recognize an individual right to bear arms.

In May 2003, the full Ninth Circuit denied a motion to set aside the panel's opinion and rehear the case. Four judges dissented from this decision, however, and the dissenting opinion written by one of the judges in particular gives us a startling view into the devious and traitorous tactics used by left-wing federal judges in their pathetic attempts to compensate for their "retarded sexual and emotional maturity" and reshape the United States in their own deformed image.

U.S. Circuit Judge Alex Kozinski writes:

Judges know very well how to read the Constitution broadly when they are sympathetic to the right being asserted. We have held, without much ado, that "speech, or . . . the press" also means the Internet, and that "persons, houses, papers, and effects" also means public telephone booths. When a particular right comports especially well with our notions of good social policy, we build magnificent legal edifices on elliptical constitutional phrases—or even the white spaces between lines of constitutional text. But, as the panel amply demonstrates, when we're none too keen on a particular constitutional guarantee, we can be equally ingenious in burying language that is incontrovertibly there.

It is wrong to use some constitutional provisions as spring-boards for major social change while treating others like senile relatives to be cooped up in a nursing home until they quit annoying us. As guardians of the Constitution, we must be consistent in interpreting its

provisions. If we adopt a jurisprudence sympathetic to individual rights, we must give broad compass to all constitutional provisions that protect individuals from tyranny. If we take a more statist approach, we must give all such provisions narrow scope. Expanding some to gargantuan proportions while discarding others like a crumpled gum wrapper is not faithfully applying the Constitution; it's using our power as federal judges to constitutionalize our personal preferences.

The able judges of the panel majority are usually very sympathetic to individual rights, but they have succumbed to the temptation to pick and choose. Had they brought the same generous approach to the Second Amendment that they routinely bring to the First, Fourth and selected portions of the Fifth, they would have had no trouble finding an individual right to bear arms. Indeed, to conclude otherwise, they had to ignore binding precedent. *United States v. Miller* (1939) did not hold that the defendants lacked standing to raise a Second Amendment defense, even though the government argued the collective rights theory in its brief. The Supreme Court reached the Second Amendment claim and rejected it on the merits after finding no evidence that Miller's weapon—a sawed-off shotgun—was reasonably susceptible to militia use. We are bound not only by the outcome of Miller but also by its rationale. If Miller's claim was dead on arrival because it was raised by a person rather than a state, why would the Court have bothered discussing whether a sawed-off shotgun was suitable for militia use? The panel majority not only ignores Miller's test; it renders most of the opinion wholly superfluous. As an inferior court, we may not tell the Supreme Court it was out to lunch when it last visited a constitutional provision.

The majority falls prey to the delusion—popular in some circles—that ordinary people are too careless and stupid to own guns, and we would be far better off leaving all weapons in the hands of professionals on the government payroll. But the simple truth—born of experience—is that tyranny thrives best where government need not fear the wrath of an armed people. Our own sorry history bears this out: Disarmament was the tool of choice for subjugating both slaves and free blacks in the South. In Florida, patrols searched blacks' homes for weapons, confiscated those found and punished their owners without judicial process. In the North, by contrast, blacks exercised their right to bear arms to defend against racial mob violence. As Chief Justice Taney well appreciated, the institution of slavery required a class of people who lacked the means to resist. See *Dred Scott v. Sandford*, (1857) (finding black citizenship unthinkable because it would give blacks the right to "keep and carry arms wherever they went"). A revolt by Nat Turner and a few dozen other armed blacks could be put down without much difficulty; one by four million armed blacks would have meant big trouble.

All too many of the other great tragedies of history—Stalin's atrocities, the killing fields of Cambodia, the Holocaust, to name but a few—were perpetrated by armed troops against unarmed populations. Many could well have been avoided or mitigated had the perpetrators known their intended victims were equipped with a rifle and twenty bullets apiece, as the Militia Act required here. If a few hundred Jewish fighters in the Warsaw Ghetto could hold off the Wehrmacht for almost a month with only a handful of weapons, six million Jews armed with rifles could not so easily have been herded into cattle cars.

My excellent colleagues have forgotten these bitter lessons of history. The prospect of tyranny may not grab the headlines the way vivid stories of gun crime routinely do. But few saw the Third Reich coming until it was too late. The Second Amendment is a doomsday provision, one designed for those exceptionally rare circumstances where all other rights have failed—where the government refuses to stand for reelection and silences those who protest; where courts have lost the courage to oppose, or can find no one to enforce their decrees. However improbable these contingencies may seem today, facing them unprepared is a mistake a free people get to make only once.

Fortunately, the Framers were wise enough to entrench the right of the people to keep and bear arms within our constitutional structure. The purpose and importance of that right was still fresh in their minds, and they spelled it out clearly so it would not be forgotten. Despite the panel's mighty struggle to erase these words, they remain, and the people themselves can read what they say plainly enough:

*A well regulated Militia, being necessary to the security of a free State, the right of the people to keep and bear Arms, shall not be infringed.*

The sheer ponderousness of the panel's opinion—the mountain of verbiage it must deploy to explain away these fourteen short words of constitutional text [the right of the people to keep and bear Arms shall not be infringed]—refutes its thesis far more convincingly than anything I might say. The panel's labored effort to smother the Second Amendment by sheer body weight has all the grace of a sumo wrestler trying to kill a rattlesnake by sitting on it— and is just as likely to succeed.